T0353724

UNDERSTANDING THE BOOK OF
PROVERBS

DR. GILBERT H. EDWARDS, SR.

authorHOUSE®

AuthorHouse™
1663 Liberty Drive
Bloomington, IN 47403
www.authorhouse.com
Phone: 833-262-8899

Published by AuthorHouse 12/13/2024

ISBN: 979-8-8230-4005-1 (sc)
ISBN: 979-8-8230-4004-4 (e)

PREFACE

Wisdom is a Godly quality endowed by the Almighty God to individuals. The Book of Proverbs should be read at least once a year. If a person listens to Proverbs with a sound mind, they will obtain a disciplined character. There are three words in the Book of Proverbs that stand out to me: <u>wisdom, knowledge and understanding</u>. Wisdom is having the ability to make the right or correct choices in life, when life's situations are opposing you. There must be an understanding of words; the ability to distinguish between similar ideas. This wisdom comes from God, but man must listen in-order to receive it. The purpose of this wisdom is so that man will be an intelligent person. One must fear God in-order to obtain knowledge, because the fear of God is the beginning of knowledge.

CONTENTS

INTRODUCTION

The Book of Proverbs builds good character and good character builds good behavior. In this study, the value of the Proverbs is explained, which explains wisdom, understanding and knowledge. Such others as the reward of seeking wisdom, exhortation to obedience, the beneficence of wisdom, warnings against unchastity, warnings against idleness and falsehood, the wiles of a Harlot, the excellence and eternity of wisdom, wisdom and the foolish woman, the upright and the wicked contrasted, Proverbs concerning life and conduct, precepts and warnings, comparisons and moral lessons, the wicked and righteous, the observation of Agur, admonition to a King and praise to a good woman. This is for everyone who will listen and receive it. Proverbs says, "Take heed and listen to my instructions."

PROVERBS 1

1. The Proverbs of Solomon, the son of David, King of Israel:

2. to know wisdom and instruction; to perceive the words of understanding;

3. to receive the instruction of wisdom, justice, and judgement, and equity;

4. to give subtilty to the simple, to the young man knowledge and discretion.

<u>Wisdom</u>. Knowing wisdom gives the ability to make the correct moral choices in situations that present opposing alternatives. This ability cannot be developed by man through his own resources but must be transmitted to him by God through the written and oral Torah, which in turn is transmitted to him by his teachers. Wisdom is the only way to identify and evade the traps set by the evil inclination, who like the serpent in the Garden of Eden, is very cunning. Our intellect's purpose is to build life. God's revelation is the place to begin intellectual development. We can build a disciplined and well-ordered life on that foundation.

<u>Moral instruction</u>. The ability to overcome natural tendencies and act solely based on one's better judgment in both spiritual and social realms.

<u>Words of</u> understanding. The ability to distinguish between similar ideas, or to infer one idea from another.

Moral discipline of the intellect. "Moral instruction" refers to an individual's desire to act in accordance with God's will because of his fear of heavenly punishment, while "moral discipline of the intellect" refers to the desire to act in accordance with His will because of one's awe of God. This higher level of devotion can only be reached through the intellect's capacity to meditate upon the secrets of creation and the profound of the upper worlds; or "moral instruction" refers to the theoretical aspects of attaining moral discipline theoretical aspects of attaining moral discipline through self-affliction while "moral discipline of the intellect" refers to its successful practical application. A person must recognize his limits and act in accordance with his natural disposition. If he afflicts himself excessively, he will gain nothing from the process.

Righteousness, in both spiritual and social realms. Meaning of conveys the quality of going beyond the letter of the Law. Just as God is compassionate, so must you be compassionate.

Justice. Referring to a Judge's capacity to formulate an impartial verdict strictly according to the letter of the Law.

Straightforwardness. Referring to the quality of being honest with others, or to reach a balance between kindness and strictness.

For providing. After mastering the study and application of moral instruction, the next step is to teach his knowledge to others.

5. A wise man will hear, and will increase learning; and a man of understanding shall attain unto wise counsels:

6. to understand a Proverb, and the interpretation; the words of the wise, and their dark saying.

Proverb and moral. "Proverb" refers to the episodes recorded in the written Torah, the story of Adam, Eve and the serpent, whereas "moral" refers to their hidden spiritual meaning.

Words of the wise and their riddles. Referring to the etymological method by which determines the meaning of certain verses in the Torah or, to the enigmatic parables that constitutes a fair portion of the oral Torah.

7. The fear of the Lord is the beginning of knowledge, "but fools despise wisdom and instruction. God is the starting point for the education that leads to wisdom. True knowledge in the biblical sense is something more than a collection of factual information. It includes knowing how to conduct oneself in the practical affairs of everyday life, to make wise choices, to do the right thing in relation to others, and to have insight into the true nature of things. Wisdom of this kind can only grow out of an awareness of God and His purpose in the world.

8. My son, hear the instruction of thy father, and forsake not the law of thy mother;

9. For they shall be an ornament of grace unto thy head, and chains about thy neck.

Heed the moral instruction. "The moral instruction of your father" alludes to the oral and written Torah that God gave Moses at Sinai, while "the teaching of your mother" alludes to the rabbinical decrees designed to prevent people from transgressing Torah Laws. The first and most important classroom in the school of life is the home. Both father and mother are expected to assume responsibility for training and nurturing the minds of children.

Head . . . throat. The head represents the intellect, the throat – the linguistic faculty. Both are perfected by moral instruction and Torah teaching.

10. My son, if sinners entice thee consent, thou not.

11. If they say come with us, let us lay wait for blood, let us lurk privily for the innocent without cause:

12. let us swallow them up alive as the grave; and whole, as those that go down into the pit;

13. we shall find all precious substance; we shall fill our houses with spoil;

14. cast in the lot among us; let us all have one purse:

15. my son, walk not thou in the way with them; refrain thy foot from their path;

16. for their feet run to evil and make haste to shed blood.

17. Surely in vain the net is spread in the sight of any bird.

18. And they lay wait for their own blood; they lurk privily for their own lives.

19. So are the ways of everyone that is greedy of gain; which taketh away the life of the owners thereof.

<u>My son, if sinners . . .</u> This is the first practical lesson that the master of Proverbs teaches his disciple. For the sake of thoroughness, he begins with a moral lesson that is self-evident even to a young child, but gradually the subtlety of his teachings increases. Stepping over God's moral limits is suicide.

<u>whole</u> – while they are in the best of health.

<u>means nothing</u> – That is "presents no threat." From the air the bird sees only the bait spread over the net, and so lands on the ground unsuspectingly. Likewise, the only thing the thieves see is the loot that will soon be theirs. Little do they realize that these very crimes will ultimately become their pitfall.

<u>hunters</u> – who spread the net and set the bait.

<u>He takes the life of its owner.</u> Thieves will murder their victims in order to keep their crimes a secret.

<u>It takes</u> – "Referring to the stolen object." "Its owner" thus refers to the thief himself, who, by stealing this object, has now become its new owner. This teaches that a thief's crimes will bring about his own downfall.

20. Wisdom crieth without; she uttereth her voice in the street;

21. she crieth in the chief place of concourse in the openings of the gates: in the city she uttereth her words, saying,

22. how long, ye simple ones, will ye love simplicity? And the scorners and fools hate knowledge?

23. Turn ye at my reproof: behold, I will pour out my spirit unto you, I will make known my words unto you.

24. Because I have called, and ye refused; I have stretched out my hand, and no man regardeth;

25. but ye have set at naught all my counsel, and would none of my reproof:

26. I also will laugh at your calamity; I will mock when your fear cometh.

27. When your fear cometh as desolation, and your destruction cometh as a whirlwind; when distress and anguish cometh upon you;

28. then shall they call upon me, but I will not answer; they shall seek me early, but they shall not find me:

29. For that they hated knowledge and did not choose the fear of the Lord:

30. they would none of my counsel: they despised all of my reproof.

31. Therefore, shall they eat of the fruit of their own way, and be filled with their own devices.

32. For the turning away of the simple shall slay them, and the prosperity of fools shall destroy them.

33. But whoso harkeneth unto me shall dwell safely and shall be quiet from fear of evil.

Wisdom cries aloud. Referring to the Torah, unlike the evil inclination which "gets an ambush" and "lies in wait" for its victims. Torah openly declares its message to anyone who will lend an ear.

In Proverbs, God's wisdom is pictured as a woman walking the streets of Jerusalem seeking to win people away from the alluring street walkers.

Simple ones. Those who are easily led astray by heretics, or their hunger for physical pleasures, or simple minded, in the sense that they get carried away by their own thoughts and act impetuously. Verse 22 urges them to protect themselves against falling prey to further deception by acquiring wisdom.

Scorners. People who are only willing to accept logical demonstrable wisdom. They scoff at the wisdom of the Torah, because unlike other disciplines, faith and fear of God are two of its most intrinsic components.

Fools. Those who know the principles of wisdom but renounce them because they interfere with the physical desires, or people who find Torah study difficult, yet are unwilling to exert their minds. When Torah knowledge fails to penetrate of its own accord, they become dejected and renounce their faith.

Refuse to listen to my words. Wisdom constantly speaks directly from within the inner recesses of a person's soul, urging him to make some effort to acquire wisdom and knowledge.

I will not answer. The loss of wisdom is a gradual process. God will not answer those who willfully reject Him.

PROVERBS 2

1. My son, if thou wilt receive my words, and hide my commandments with thee;

2. so that thou incline thine ear unto wisdom, and apply thine heart to understanding;

3. yea, if thou criest after knowledge, and liftest up thy voice for understanding;

4. if thou seekest her as silver, and searchest for her as for hid treasures;

5. then shalt thou understand the fear of the Lord, and find the knowledge of God.

Wisdom is the gift of God. Those who accept His wisdom will find it a firm basis for understanding His revelation, as well as all of life's knowledge.

Listen to wisdom. To arrive at true wisdom man must "make his ear listen"; receive it in the form of an oral transmission from his teacher, who in turn receives it from previous generations dating back to Moses and the prophets.

Seek it as you do silver. To attain, be willing to far and wide in the pursuit of Torah, just as people are willing to wonder from place to place in order to earn a living.

<u>Hidden treasures</u>. The quest for wisdom requires delving deeply into the words of the sages and extracting the esoteric teachings that they encompass.

6. For the LORD giveth wisdom: out of his mouth cometh knowledge and understanding.

7. He layeth up sound wisdom for the righteous: he is a buckler to them that walk uprightly.

8. He keepeth the paths of judgment, and preserveth the way of his saints.

9. Then shalt thou understand righteousness, and judgment, and equity; yea, every good path.

<u>God gives wisdom. . . His mouth.</u> The knowledge that all wisdom emanates from God is enough reason to strive to attain it.

<u>Everlasting wisdom</u>. The Torah's esoteric teachings which God stored away solely for the righteous.

<u>Path . . . ways . . .</u> The way of life. Wisdom comes from God and has the ability to rescue people from evil choices and poor decisions. God can speak through the awakened mind and the imagination of the believer. God not only uses the mind in dreams and visions at night or in an event that communicates His will, but He also gives insight to the average individual in reading and reflection on His truth (Psalm 145:5).

<u>Every good path.</u> "A winding trail." In confrontations with the wicked, it is sometimes necessary to veer from the "straight road" of exemplary behavior and temporarily tread a "winding course" of negative character traits.

10. When wisdom entereth into thine heart, and knowledge is pleasant unto thy soul;

11. discretion shall preserve thee, understanding shall keep thee:

12. to deliver thee from the way of the evil man, from the man that speaketh froward things;

13. who leave the paths of uprightness, to walk in the ways of darkness;

14. who rejoice to do evil, and delight in the frowardness of the wicked;

15. whose ways are crooked, and they froward in their paths:

16. to deliver thee from the strange woman, even from the stranger which flattereth with her words;

17. which forsaketh the guide of her youth, and forgetteth the covenant of her God.

<u>Enter your heart . . .</u> The wisdom that God bestows usurps the Evil Inclination's role as primary force determining one's deeds, thus effectively ending the internal struggle between one's opposing inclinations.

<u>Prudence . . . discernment . . .</u> Refers to the Torah study, which protects one from impure thoughts, and also refer to the faculty of discernment spawned by Torah study, which guards one from actively transgressing

18. For her house inclineth unto death, and her paths unto the dead.

19. None that go unto her return again, neither take they hold of the paths of life.

20. That thou mayest walk in the way of good men and keep the paths of the righteous.

21. For the upright shall dwell in the land, and the perfect shall remain in it.

22. But the wicked shall be cut off from the earth and the transgressors shall be rooted out of it.

<u>Her house . . . Death</u>; her house is like a corridor that leads to death; whoever enters falls into the abyss.

<u>Do not return</u>; they will find it excruciatingly difficult to part from her. Those who entertain heretical beliefs will not return to the ways of the Torah. Even if they should decide to repent, the heresy works within them like yeast in dough, so that they will never find their way back to wholehearted faith.

<u>So that you may walk</u>: "It will save you . . . so that you may walk."

<u>The good . . . the righteous</u>; many people are "good" and give to the needy, but few are "righteous" who give freely even to those undeserving of assistance.

<u>Wicked . . . treacherous</u>; "the wicked" are those who transgress against God and society, whereas "the treacherous" transgress only against their fellow man.

PROVERBS 3

1. My son, forget not my law; but let thine heart keep my commandments:

2. For length of days, and long life, and peace, shall they add to thee.

3. Let not mercy and truth forsake thee: bind them about thy neck; write them upon the table of thine heart:

4. So shalt thou find favour and good understanding in the sight of God and man.

The wisdom teacher assumed the role of Father to his students and tried to motivate them to learn and put into practice his teachings. Obeying the inspired teaching of scripture develops character which pleases both God and other people.

Do not forget. One accomplishes this by studying all areas of Torah, including those with no practical application today, as well as the Torah's narratives, which contain the basic tenets of faith in God: Divine provident, the Holy origin of prophecy, and reward and punishment.

Length of days, years of life, and peace. "Length of days" refers to quality of life of days filled with good; "years of life" means a long life-in merit of a person's Torah study where he is granted additional years of life; "peace" refers to health, prosperity and domestic harmony.

Bind them about your throat. The throat is the source of speech; hence, "bind them about your throat" means to speak of them constantly, so that they become second nature to you.

Inscribe them on the table of your heart. Being the center for one's emotions, the heart is constantly bombarded by physical desires and illicit fantasies, which contradict the dictums of wisdom. The verse urges one to incorporate the tenets of wisdom into the depths of one's being, so that it should serve as a signpost to guide one well away from these pitfalls.

Grace and higher intelligence. . . There are qualitative differences between wisdom attained through Torah study and that attained solely on the basis of human resources. Both brings the bearer social recognition, but only through Torah can one "find grace in the eyes of the Lord", as well; both result in the bearer achieving a high level of intelligence, but only through Torah study can one reach "high intelligence", a synonym for divine inspiration.

5. Trust in the LORD with all thine heart; and lean not unto thine own understanding.

6. In all thy ways acknowledge him, and he shall direct thy paths.

7. Be not wise in thine own eyes: fear the LORD, and depart from evil.

8. It shall be health to thy navel, and marrow to thy bones.

God directs the paths of those who wholeheartedly trust in Him.

Do not be wise. . . Do not scoff at those who rebuke you or do not consider yourself exempt from rabbinical prohibitions designed to prevent the people from violating Torah Law.

Cure for your flesh. In verse 8, the "bones" represent the positive commandments and the "flesh", the prohibitions. "It" refers to the last clause of the previous verse – "turning away from evil", or repentance. By repenting for one's sins, a person can rectify or cure the spiritual damage he has caused to the different elements of his body.

9. Honour the LORD with thy substance, and with the firstfruits of all thine increase:

10. so shall thy barns be filled with plenty, and thy presses shall burst out with new wine.

11. My son, despise not the chastening of the LORD; neither be weary of his correction:

12. for whom the LORD loveth he correcteth; even as a father the son in whom he delighteth.

<u>Son in whom He delighteth.</u> The experience of God's people through the years is distilled into a pithy proverb by the inspired writer. It shows that God's people can count on His blessings when we honor Him with our offerings. As with all proverbial wisdom, this is not an ironclad rule without exceptions. It is a principle proved through experience and inspired by God.

<u>With the first fruits . . .</u> "by separating tithes" Deuteronomy 26:2.

<u>God's chastisement.</u> One must accept personal tragedy with love and understanding., For when God takes the trouble to chastise a person, it is only because He truly care for him.

<u>He is like a Father consoling . . .</u> As a Father comforts his son after physically punishing him, so too, God consoles those who have undergone personal grief by bestowing blessings on them. God causes a person to undergo adversity for the same reason a Father strikes his son – only to convince him to correct his ways. Therefore, one should not denigrate God's chastisement or abhor His rebuke. God is our Father who wants to teach us the wise path of life. He disciplines us in love, when we require it.

13. Happy is the man that findeth wisdom, and the man that getteth understanding.

14. For the merchandise of it is better than the merchandise of silver, and the gain thereof than fine gold.

15. She is more precious than rubies: and all the things thou canst desire are not to be compared unto her.

16. Length of days is in her right hand; and in her left-hand riches and honour.

17. Her ways are ways of pleasantness, and all her paths are peace.

18. She is a tree of life to them that lay hold upon her: and happy is every one that retaineth her.

Wisdom is knowing the way of the Lord. Wisdom comes through experience with God in His world and includes experiencing His discipline. Those who find wisdom and gain understanding are blessed. Wisdom here means knowledge of the moral law of God, as it concerns the practical affairs of life. True wisdom promotes health, well-being, and happiness. Many of the problems that plague human existence spring from poor judgement, foolish choices, and refused values. God given wisdom helps us to avoid these pitfalls and heightens the quality of life.

Finds wisdom . . . derives discernment. Wisdom, not generated by man's own resources, but bestowed by God, is "found"; conversely, discernment, determined by each man's intellectual capacity is "derived" from empirical data.

Her trade . . . In contrast to regular commerce, when two people, "trade" for wisdom by sharing Torah knowledge with each other, both parties benefit by still retaining what they previously owned.

All that you desire . . . Dening oneself earthly desires is a prerequisite for attaining wisdom, yet wisdom's true worth is far greater than all of man's earthly desires combined.

Her ways are pleasant ways. "Her ways" refers to the general direction towards true spiritual pleasure, or "her ways" refers to the general direction towards which Torah observance leads – the emotional and spiritual serenity experienced by those aware of the true purpose of their existence.

19. The Lord by wisdom hath founded the earth; by understanding hath he established the heavens.

20. By his knowledge the depths are broken up, and the clouds drop down the dew.

God's wisdom directs His mighty acts of creation, making creation very good. Creation has purpose and meaning. Divine wisdom guided each step of the universe's origin. Nothing was accidental or opposed to God's wise purpose. The wisdom behind creation proves the wisdom of letting divine wisdom guide each of life's choices.

Depths were burst open. Referring to underground water sources.

21. My son, let not them depart from thine eyes: keep sound wisdom and discretion:

22. So shall they be life unto thy soul, and grace to thy neck.

23. Then shalt thou walk in thy way safely, and thy foot shall not stumble.

24. When thou liest down, thou shalt not be afraid: yea, thou shalt lie down, and thy sleep shall be sweet.

25. Be not afraid of sudden fear, neither of the desolation of the wicked, when it cometh.

26. For the Lord shall be thy confidence and shall keep thy foot from being taken.

27. Withhold not good from them to whom it is due, when it is in the power of thine hand to do it.

28. Say not unto thy neighbor, go, and come again, and tomorrow I will give; when thou hast it by thee.

<u>Dark destruction . . .</u> Even if you find yourself in the midst of a "dark destruction" know that it has come in order to punish the wicked, and trust that you will be saved by means of Divine providence.

<u>The one who deserves it.</u> The poor.

<u>When you have it.</u> The verse warns against delaying payment of a hired worker.

29. Devise not evil against thy neighbor, seeing he dwelleth securely by thee.

30. Strive not with a man without cause, if he have done thee no harm.

31. Envy thou not the oppressor, and choose none of his ways.

32. For the froward is abomination to the LORD: but his secret is with the righteous.

33. The curse of the LORD is in the house of the wicked: but he blesseth the habitation of the just.

34. Surely, he scorneth the scorners: but he giveth grace unto the lowly.

35. The wise shall inherit glory: but shame shall be the promotion of fools.

<u>For no reason.</u> So not quarrel even with someone who caused you harm, if you will accomplish nothing by doing so.

<u>Or choose any of his ways.</u> Do not emulate even his positive traits, for "even the good of the wicked is evil to the righteous."

<u>His private counsel is with the upright.</u> God reveals to the righteous when an how He will punish the wicked (Genesis 18:17).

<u>House . . . dwelling . . .</u> "House" conveys a solid edifice, whereas "dwelling" conveys a temporary shelter, such as a tent. Despite their flimsy dwellings, the righteous will prosper, whereas the solid homes of the wicked will fail to protect them against God's curse. So too, in the world to come, the righteous will be blessed and the wicked cursed.

PROVERBS 4

1. Hear, ye children, the instruction of a father, and attend to know understanding.

2. For I give you good doctrine, forsake ye not my law.

3. For I was my father's son, tender and only beloved in the sight of my mother.

4. He taught me also, and said unto me, Let thine heart retain my words: keep my commandments, and live.

Life needs goals. Two major alternatives face us; obedience to God and dedication to evil. Those on evil's path deserve the punishment that comes.

I was once . . . A person must rise above his earthly desires and strive for loftier ideals. The writer exhorts one to overcome human nature and forgo those things which the senses naturally crave, such as immoral sex conduct and theft.

Let my words brace your heart. Moral instruction prevents the heart from swaying to and fro with the winds of physical desire and passion. Instead, it keeps the heart fixed on the path of wisdom. "Instruction" refers to a process of training in which the learner submits to the teaching and guidance of a wiser person. To benefit from such instruction, we must cultivate a teachable spirit and accept the discipline of firm guidance. The ultimate reward of such training will be a long and useful life.

5. Get wisdom, get understanding: forget it not; neither decline from the words of my mouth.

6. Forsake her not, and she shall preserve thee: love her, and she shall keep thee.

7. Wisdom is the principal thing; therefore, get wisdom: and with all thy getting get understanding.

8. Exalt her, and she shall promote thee: she shall bring thee to honour, when thou dost embrace her.

9. She shall give to thine head an ornament of grace: a crown of glory shall she deliver to thee.

10. Hear, O my son, and receive my sayings; and the years of thy life shall be many.

Acquire wisdom, knowledge and understanding. If no one is willing to teach you Torah for free, then hire a teacher, for you cannot arrive at wisdom independently. If no one is willing to study together with you, then hire a study partner with whom to analyze your lesson, for this is the only way to acquire true understanding.

The beginning of wisdom . . . The first step in the process of attaining wisdom is to find a suitable teacher.

11. I have taught thee in the way of wisdom; I have led thee in right paths.

12. When thou goest, thy steps shall not be straitened; and when thou runnest, thou shalt not stumble.

13. Take fast hold of instruction; let her not go: keep her; for she is thy life.

14. Enter not into the path of the wicked, and go not in the way of evil men.

15. Avoid it, pass not by it, turn from it, and pass away.

When you walk in the path of wisdom, your steps will not be hindered.

<u>Your steps will not be hindered . . . not stumble.</u> At first, the service of God is an arduous process. Progress comes slowly, with the individual moving forward from one spiritual level to the next in excruciatingly small increments. The obstacles in his path are numerous and often extremely painful. This verse teaches that one who studies Torah will receive divine assistance, and that eventually, he will succeed in attaining his spiritual goal. When you walk, do not take small steps, when you run, do not stumble.

<u>It is your life.</u> Man was only given life so that he can overcome his negative traits. A person must always improve, for if he does not, what is his justification for living?

16. For they sleep not, except they have done mischief; and their sleep is taken away, unless they cause some to fall.

17. For they eat the bread of wickedness, and drink the wine of violence.

18. But the path of the just is as the shining light, that shineth more and more unto the perfect day.

19. The way of the wicked is as darkness: they know not at what they stumble.

20. My son, attend to my words; incline thine ear unto my sayings.

21. Let them not depart from thine eyes; keep them in the midst of thine heart.

<u>They do not know what will make them stumble.</u> They commit transgressions even when they do not intend to so.

<u>Sight . . . your heart.</u> "Sight" alludes to written Torah, which is studied with the eyes; "incline your ear" in verse 20 alludes to oral Torah, which is studied with one's voice. "Your heart" alludes to the esoteric teachings of the Torah, which can only be understood with the heart.

22. For they are life unto those that find them, and health to all their flesh.

23. Keep thy heart with all diligence; for out of it are the issues of life.

24. Put away from thee a froward mouth, and perverse lips put far from thee.

25. Let thine eyes look right on, and let thine eyelids look straight before thee.

26. Ponder the path of thy feet, and let all thy ways be established.

27. Turn not to the right hand nor to the left: remove thy foot from evil.

<u>Whatever you guard. . .</u> The verse warns against contemplating sinful thoughts, guard your heart from all forms of captivity, and especially from the iron grip of physical desires.

<u>Crooked mouth . . . twisted lips.</u> Make certain that you conduct does not give people reason to make disapproving facial gestures in your presence.

<u>Let your eyes look forward,</u> and perceive truth, so that you may plan your life wisely. Always choose the middle path in life and keep away from extremes.

<u>Your pupils gaze straight ahead,</u> that they may lead you to rectify your ways and choose the straight path. Your eyelids . . . regarding spiritual

matters, your eyes should be wide open and "looking forward", but when it comes to physical desires, you should close your eyes tightly and let your eyelids – not your eyes – gage ahead.

<u>Evaluate . . .</u> During the decision-making process, weigh the advantages and disadvantages of violating a commandment against those of observing it. If you do this, "all your ways will be set firm."

PROVERBS 5

1. My son, attend unto my wisdom, and bow thine ear to my understanding.

2. That thou mayest regard discretion, and that thy lips may keep knowledge.

3. For the lips of a strange woman drop as an honeycomb, and her mouth is smoother than oil:

4. But her end is bitter as wormwood, sharp as a two-edged sword.

5. Her feet go down to death; her steps take hold on hell.

6. Lest thou shouldest ponder the path of life, her ways are moveable, that thou canst not know them.

Wisdom warns against conceding to a very strong, but temporary desire that has long-term, destructive results. Adultery is specifically identified, but all infidelity appears to being implied as being the kind of life which leads to death. Living only to satisfy the pleasures of the flesh is the way of folly. Eventually, moral corruption robs us of the ability to distinguish right from wrong.

Double-edged sword. Just as it kills with both edges, so the female stranger causes one to lose both this world and the next.

<u>Her steps support nether world.</u> Figuratively, she sustains the nether world by supplying it with the souls of her victims.

<u>Do not evaluate . . .</u> Do not attempt to rationally choose between eternal life and the enticements of the female stranger, for before you know it, her shifting courses will have let you down to death. Do not attempt to estimate how you can follow her and still remain safely on the path of life, for as scripture says, "all who go to her do not return, nor will they attain the paths of life. (2:19) – her shifting course will cause you to lose your bearing and not find your way back.

7. Hear me now therefore, O ye children, and depart not from the words of my mouth.

8. Remove thy way far from her, and come not nigh the door of her house:

9. Lest thou give thine honour unto others, and thy years unto the cruel:

10. Lest strangers be filled with thy wealth; and thy labours be in the house of a stranger;

11. And thou mourn at the last, when thy flesh and thy body are consumed,

12. And say, How have I hated instruction, and my heart despised reproof;

13. And have not obeyed the voice of my teachers, nor inclined mine ear to them that instructed me!

14. I was almost in all evil in the midst of the congregation and assembly.

<u>Lest you give your praise to others.</u> Under the influence of the female stranger, you will direct your praise to idols instead of to God. Lest you

relinquish your splendor to others – under her influence, the glory that God bestows upon every living being will be removed from you and given to someone else.

<u>Lest strangers . . .</u> Lest all your money go to priests of idolatry.

<u>A stranger's home.</u> In temple of idol worship.

<u>Trifling:</u> Referring to earthly pleasures among a congregation and an assembly. A sinner's transgressions will be made public to a large congregation of people, and his punishment will be administered in the presence of an assembly of righteous individuals.

15. Drink waters out of thine own cistern, and running waters out of thine own well.

16. Let thy fountains be dispersed abroad, and rivers of waters in the streets.

17. Let them be only thine own, and not strangers' with thee.

18. Let thy fountain be blessed: and rejoice with the wife of thy youth.

19. Let her be as the loving hind and pleasant roe; let her breasts satisfy thee at all times; and be thou ravished always with her love.

20. And why wilt thou, my son, be ravished with a strange woman, and embrace the bosom of a stranger?

21. For the ways of man are before the eyes of the Lord, and he pondereth all his goings.

22. His own iniquities shall take the wicked himself, and he shall be holden with the cords of his sins.

23. He shall die without instruction; and in the greatness of his folly he shall go astray.

<u>So drink . . .</u> Draw guidance from the Torah which God gave to you, rather than from alien sources.

<u>Your springs.</u> The reward to be earned by those who paid attention to instruction: their wisdom will progressively increase and ultimately it will overflow and reach great numbers of disciples in every direction. They will merit having children who will become famous for their great wisdom.,

<u>Infatuated with love for her.</u> Uninterrupted Torah study inadvertently err due to your love for her – spending an inordinate amount of time with one's wife draws one away from the service of God.

<u>He evaluates his every course.</u> God weighs each person's worthy deeds against his transgressions, and He rewards or punishes accordingly. A person ought not delude himself into believing that there are pure motives behind his pursuit of earthly desires, for God knows the truth.

<u>He will be held . . .</u> His own transgressions will become the rope from which he will be hanged. In this sense, the rope "holds" or lifts the body of the condemned man.

PROVERBS 6

1. My son, if thou be surety for thy friend, if thou hast stricken thy hand with a stranger,

2. Thou art snared with the words of thy mouth, thou art taken with the words of thy mouth.

3. Do this now, my son, and deliver thyself, when thou art come into the hand of thy friend; go, humble thyself, and make sure thy friend.

4. Give not sleep to thine eyes, nor slumber to thine eyelids.

5. Deliver thyself as a roe from the hand of the hunter, and as a bird from the hand of the fowler.

Our tongue can get us into trouble. We may agree without thinking to a contract made by a dishonest person. When we recognize the wrongness of our attitudes and words, we need to act immediately. We must not quit, until we are reconciled to the other person and nullify the agreement. In so doing, we must admit our wrongness.

Giving your handshake to a stranger. To a moneylender, or given your handshake on behalf of a stranger, you have become caught and ensnared by the words of your own mouth.

Humble yourself . . . exalt your fellow man. So that he will release you from your pledge.

From the hand of the hunter; "from the trap"

6. Go to the ant, thou sluggard; consider her ways, and be wise:

7. Which having no guide, overseer, or ruler,

8. Provideth her meat in the summer, and gathereth her food in the harvest.

No one should have to force us to work. Planning for the future and hard work in the present are the basics for life. These, however, are also expected to be coupled with cooperative relations with those around us.

Store up its food; Man, as a microcosm of the entire creation embodies all the forces in nature. In order to remind mankind of its vast potential, God instilled many species of animals with traits that are clearly unnecessary for their survival. For example, the ant. It lives twelve months during which time it eat no more than kernels of wheat in numbers that far exceed the needs of the entire colony. The ant's tireless toil for food is a poignant lesson that a person should never feel satisfied with the amount of Torah he knows, but should always strive to acquire more wisdom.

9. How long wilt thou sleep, O sluggard? when wilt thou arise out of thy sleep?

10. Yet a little sleep, a little slumber, a little folding of the hands to sleep:

11. So shall thy poverty come as one that travelleth, and thy want as an armed man.

12. A naughty person, a wicked man, walketh with a froward mouth.

13. He winketh with his eyes, he speaketh with his feet, he teacheth with his fingers;

14. Frowardness is in his heart, he deviseth mischief continually; he soweth discord.

15. Therefore shall his calamity come suddenly; suddenly shall he be broken without remedy.

16. These six things doth the Lord hate: yea, seven are an abomination unto him:

17. A proud look, a lying tongue, and hands that shed innocent blood,

18. An heart that deviseth wicked imaginations, feet that be swift in running to mischief,

19. A false witness that speaketh lies, and he that soweth discord among brethren.

Sin has one reward – destruction, death. To earn the reward, you simply use filthy language, give deceitful or cheating gestures, plan how to take advantage of other people, create controversy, be proud, lie, murder, testify falsely and stir up every possible evil. All represent sin against the community. They break God's guidelines for life, and He will punish the sinner.

He goes with a twisted mouth; with these physical gestures, he beckons others to sin, to participate in idol worship, or through these gestures he surreptitiously slanders others.

One who foments discord between brothers; by speaking slander. This is the worst sin of all because the other six harm only two-the culprit and the victim – while this transgression harms three – the slanderer, the slandered and the listener.

20. My son, keep thy father's commandment, and forsake not the law of thy mother:

21. Bind them continually upon thine heart, and tie them about thy neck.

22. When thou goest, it shall lead thee; when thou sleepest, it shall keep thee; and when thou awakest, it shall talk with thee.

23. For the commandment is a lamp; and the law is light; and reproofs of instruction are the way of life:

24. To keep thee from the evil woman, from the flattery of the tongue of a strange woman.

25. Lust not after her beauty in thine heart; neither let her take thee with her eyelids.

26. For by means of a whorish woman a man is brought to a piece of bread: and the adultress will hunt for the precious life.

27. Can a man take fire in his bosom, and his clothes not be burned?

28. Can one go upon hot coals, and his feet not be burned?

29. So he that goeth in to his neighbour's wife; whosoever toucheth her shall not be innocent.

When you lie down; when you lie down to sleep or when you lie down in the grave.

Talk with you; in the warm and informal manner that people use when speaking to a good friend.

Moral rebuke is the path of life: Just as a man might chastise his child, so God your Lord is chastising you and for God your Lord is bringing you to a good land . . . "And from where do we know that the next world is only acquired through hardship?" (Deuteronomy 8:5,7)

<u>The evil woman:</u> The verse refers to a prostitute. In the context of verse 23, this would imply that the entire purpose of the Torah is to protect one from the enticements of harlots and no more. "The evil woman" must represent idolatry, the worst of all sins, mankind's physical desires, or the fields of study that could lead to heresy.

<u>For on account of a harlot . . .</u> the harlot represents man's physical desire, the bread represents the Torah. The verse teaches that if a person pursues the fulfillment of his physical desires, he will eventually forget all the Torah he knows.

<u>A married woman . . .</u> an unchaste married woman has the ability to lure even a righteous person to sin. Thereby, trapping him in Gehinnom.

30. Men do not despise a thief, if he steal to satisfy his soul when he is hungry;

31. But if he be found, he shall restore sevenfold; he shall give all the substance of his house.

32. But whoso committeth adultery with a woman lacketh understanding he that doeth it destroyeth his own soul.

33. A wound and dishonour shall he get; and his reproach shall not be wiped away.

34. For jealousy is the rage of a man: therefore, he will not spare in the day of vengeance.

35. He will not regard any ransom; neither will he rest content, though thou givest many gifts.

Parental teaching helps young adults avoid tragic mistakes. Among such tragedies is the disaster of sexual sins with immoral women and wayward wives. Such sins brings with flirtatious looks and end with disastrous punishments. Shame, disgrace and revenge chart life's course for the adulterer. Sex brings true joy and pleasure only within marriage.

PROVERBS 7

1. My son, keep my words, and lay up my commandments with thee.

2. Keep my commandments, and live; and my law as the apple of thine eye.

3. Bind them upon thy fingers, write them upon the table of thine heart.

4. Say unto wisdom, Thou art my sister; and call understanding thy kinswoman:

5. That they may keep thee from the strange woman, from the stranger which flattereth with her words.

Instructions in the Word of God and a serious commitment to live by it provides a safeguard against moral lapses.

Say to wisdom . . . Become as familiar with wisdom and understanding as with your closest relatives.

It will protect you: Just as one would dissuade a blood-relation from committing an evil deed.

6. For at the window of my house I looked through my casement,

7. and beheld among the simple ones, I discerned among the youths, a young man void of understanding,

8. Passing through the street near her corner; and he went the way to her house,

9. In the twilight, in the evening, in the black and dark night:

10. And, behold, there met him a woman with the attire of an harlot, and subtil of heart.

11. (She is loud and stubborn; her feet abide not in her house:

12. Now is she without, now in the streets, and lieth in wait at every corner.)

13. So she caught him, and kissed him, and with an impudent face said unto him,

14. I have peace offerings with me; this day have I payed my vows.

15. Therefore came I forth to meet thee, diligently to seek thy face, and I have found thee.

16. I have decked my bed with coverings of tapestry, with carved works, with fine linen of Egypt.

17. I have perfumed my bed with myrrh, aloes, and cinnamon.

18. Come, let us take our fill of love until the morning: let us solace ourselves with loves.

19. For the goodman is not at home, he is gone a long journey:

20. He hath taken a bag of money with him, and will come home at the day appointed.

Evil may be alluring and offer temporary pleasure. It never produces long term good for an individual. The young are especially susceptible to the temptation of sex outside of marriage. They often do not exercise mature judgement to consider broken life resulting from yielding to sexual allures.

<u>At dusk . . . pitch black:</u> In the evening, dusk, he passes through the marketplace, but later, in the deepest dark of night, he strides in the direction of her house.

<u>Dressed like a harlot:</u> walking like a harlot, or a scantily-dressed harlot.

<u>Out to capture hearts;</u> her heart is completely absorbed (with sinful thoughts).

<u>She is loud . . .</u> In order to arouse her patrons and lure them towards her, she is irritable and exasperating.

<u>The type that is never at home;</u> Her legs do not rest in her own house.

<u>Lie in wait.</u> For her patrons-senseless individuals who interrupt their Torah study for no good reason.

<u>I had pledged. . .</u> The harlot would lure the youth to her home by promising him a share of the peace-offering she had supposedly offered in the temple that day.

<u>For the man.</u> The harlot's use of the third person in reference to her own husband indicates her lack of loyalty toward him, or "the man" refer to God-the harlot emboldens her victim to do her bidding by telling hm that God has removed His Divine presence from the world.

21. With her much fair speech she caused him to yield, with the flattering of her lips she forced him.

22. He goeth after her straightway, as an ox goeth to the slaughter, or as a fool to the correction of the stocks;

23. Till a dart strike through his liver; as a bird hasteth to the snare, and knoweth not that it is for his life.

24. Hearken unto me now therefore, O ye children, and attend to the words of my mouth.

25. Let not thine heart decline to her ways, go not astray in her paths.

26. For she hath cast down many wounded: yea, many strong men have been slain by her.

27. Her house is the way to hell, going down to the chambers of death.

<u>Turn him aside.</u> From the righteous path.

<u>Suddenly, he follows her;</u> on his own making further enticements on the part of the evil inclination unnecessary. The word "suddenly" implies that the youth followed the harlot on the spur of the moment, against his better judgment. This is why he moves haltingly, like the ox led to the slaughterhouse, or the snake as it readies to strike.

<u>Until the arrow . . .</u> (He is hesitant.) until the arrow (of passion) pierces his liver – thereafter, he (hurries) …."

<u>Numerous . . .</u> "She has killed (even the greatest individuals – the evil inclination is capable of causing even the most righteous individuals of the generation to sin.

PROVERBS 8

1. Doth not wisdom cry? and understanding put forth her voice?

2. She standeth in the top of high places, by the way in the places of the paths.

3. She crieth at the gates, at the entry of the city, at the coming in at the doors.

4. Unto you, O men, I call; and my voice is to the sons of man.

5. O ye simple, understand wisdom: and, ye fools, be ye of an understanding heart.

6. Hear; for I will speak of excellent things; and the opening of my lips shall be right things.

7. For my mouth shall speak truth; and wickedness is an abomination to my lips.

8. All the words of my mouth are in righteousness; there is nothing froward or perverse in them.

9. They are all plain to him that understandeth, and right to them that find knowledge.

10. Receive my instruction, and not silver; and knowledge rather than choice gold.

11. For wisdom is better than rubies; and all the things that may be desired are not to be compared to it.

Wisdom viewed as a person; wisdom extends an invitation of learning to everyone she meets. She is not confined to academic halls or classrooms. She walks the streets, moves among the people and stands in crowded thoroughfares. Here is the biblical picture of the modern ideal of universal, lifelong learning, in which people can gain treasures of the mind and heart-worth for more than material resources. God wants to teach us His ways through every experience of life. This divine wisdom is offered to all who know and admit their own ignorance.

<u>O ye simple.</u> O ye simple ones; referring to those who fall prey to the enticements of the evil inclination. Acumen enables them to both recognize and sidestep these pitfalls.

<u>Learn to discipline the heart.</u> And overcome your desires.

<u>Take my moral instruction and not silver.</u> With silver one can only purchase only aterial goods, whereas with moral discipline, one can ultimately acquire wisdom.

<u>Knowledge rather than choice sold.</u> Fine gold gives pleasure only to the eyes, whereas knowledge of the divine pervades one's entire being with spiritual bliss.

12. I wisdom dwell with prudence, and find out knowledge of witty inventions.

13. The fear of the Lord is to hate evil: pride, and arrogancy, and the evil way, and the froward mouth, do I hate.

14. Counsel is mine, and sound wisdom: I am understanding; I have strength.

15. By me kings reign, and princes decree justice.

16. By me princes rule, and nobles, even all the judges of the earth.

17. I love them that love me; and those that seek me early shall find me.

18. Riches and honour are with me; yea, durable riches and righteousness.

19. My fruit is better than gold, yea, than fine gold; and my revenue than choice silver.

20. I lead in the way of righteousness, in the midst of the paths of judgment:

21. That I may cause those that love me to inherit substance; and I will fill their treasures.

Property rights – choosing to seek and follow God's wisdom lets us see wealth in proper perspective, so seeking wealth does not become the all-consuming goal of life. God's wisdom stands at the very heart of God's being. Wisdom is the basis of all God does.

Counsel . . . strength is mine. Wisdom serves a dual purpose in the battle against the evil inclination; it enables one to identify the enemy. It also provides a plan of attack and the necessary weapons to ensure a victorious campaign.

Kings reign. If a King does not observe the Laws of the Torah, his reign will not endure.

Through me . . . all righteousness judges. Only by consulting the Torah Law, Israel's leaders hope to decree just laws. The verse teaches that only individuals who are well-versed in the Torah may serve as Judges in Israel, regardless of the extent of their personal power.

My fruit is better . . . "My fruit", which presents eternal reward, "is better than gold."

I walk ... Wisdom can only be attained by one who is righteous and just.

I will bequeath .... a gift of real substance; I have plenty to bequeath to those who love me.

22. The Lord possessed me in the beginning of his way, before his works of old.

23. I was set up from everlasting, from the beginning, or ever the earth was.

24. When there were no depths, I was brought forth; when there were no fountains abounding with water.

25. Before the mountains were settled, before the hills was I brought forth:

26. While as yet he had not made the earth, nor the fields, nor the highest part of the dust of the world.

27. When he prepared the heavens, I was there: when he set a compass upon the face of the depth:

28. When he established the clouds above: when he strengthened the fountains of the deep:

29. When he gave to the sea his decree, that the waters should not pass his commandment: when he appointed the foundations of the earth:

30. Then I was by him, as one brought up with him: and I was daily his delight, rejoicing always before him;

31. Rejoicing in the habitable part of his earth; and my delights were with the sons of men.

Wisdom should be the guide and goal for life because wisdom was a possession of God in creation, is an eternal aspect of God's being, and underlies all other elements of creation. All elements are interrelated. The world is constituted in such a way that those who coo4rate with God's basic laws find the natural world sustains their life. God's natural and moral laws make sense when viewed from the Creator's wisdom. To obey these laws show good judgement.

<u>The Lord possessed me.</u> God created wisdom before He created the world.

<u>When there were no depths;</u> no deep, no springs abounding with water. The gases and liquids of Creation had not yet been separated from each other.

<u>The land and its environs.</u> The Torah was created when the large land masses were still submerged in the sea.

<u>First of the earth's dust.</u> The first civilized regions on earth; maybe it refers to Adam, or to the spirit of God the "hovered over the water's surface."

<u>Delighted with mankind;</u> The Torah is a source of delight to mankind.

32. Now therefore hearken unto me, O ye children: for blessed are they that keep my ways.

33. Hear instruction, and be wise, and refuse it not.

34. Blessed is the man that heareth me, watching daily at my gates, waiting at the posts of my doors.

35. For whoso findeth me findeth life, and shall obtain favour of the Lord.

36. But he that sinneth against me wrongeth his own soul: all they that hate me love death.

<u>Watching daily at my gates.</u> "Coming regularly" – the verse refers to those who are first to arrive at the study hall and last to leave.

PROVERBS 9

1. Wisdom hath builded her house, she hath hewn out her seven pillars:

2. She hath killed her beasts; she hath mingled her wine; she hath also furnished her table.

3. She hath sent forth her maidens: she crieth upon the highest places of the city,

4. Whoso is simple, let him turn in hither: as for him that wanteth understanding, she saith to him,

5. Come, eat of my bread, and drink of the wine which I have mingled.

<u>Her house;</u> referring to the world which God created with wisdom.

<u>Hewn her seven pillows;</u> referring to the seven days of the week.

<u>Meat . . . wine . . . table . . . ;</u> representing the written Law, the oral Law and the Talmud, respectively.

<u>Her maidens;</u> Moses, Aaron, Miriam and the prophets; or Adam and Eve.

6. Forsake the foolish, and live; and go in the way of understanding.

7. He that reproveth a scorner getteth to himself shame: and he that rebuketh a wicked man getteth himself a blot.

8. Reprove not a scorner, lest he hate thee: rebuke a wise man, and he will love thee.

9. Give instruction to a wise man, and he will be yet wiser: teach a just man, and he will increase in learning.

Long before modern educators learned of a "predisposition toward learning", the biblical writer pointed out that a wise and knowledgeable person is receptive to further instruction. Learning kindles a desire for more learning.

Humiliation . . . blemish; when admonished scoffers strike back by humiliating the person rebuking them. But when evil individuals are admonished, they respond by accusing the person rebuking them of having the same blemish as they.

He will use you. This is because to the wise, self-improvement is the most important goal.

10. The fear of the Lord is the beginning of wisdom: and the knowledge of the holy is understanding.

11. For by me thy days shall be multiplied, and the years of thy life shall be increased.

12. If thou be wise, thou shalt be wise for thyself: but if thou scornest, thou alone shalt bear it.

13. A foolish woman is clamorous: she is simple, and knoweth nothing.

14. For she sitteth at the door of her house, on a seat in the high places of the city,

15. To call passengers who go right on their ways:

16. Whoso is simple, let him turn in hither: and as for him that wanteth understanding, she saith to him,

17. Stolen waters are sweet, and bread eaten in secret is pleasant.

18. But he knoweth not that the dead are there; and that her guests are in the depths of hell.

God's wisdom, personified as a hostess, is contrasted with a foolish woman. Two forces within and without us beckon one, wisdom, invites us to dine with her and truly enjoy the benefits of the Lord. The other, folly, tempts us to destroy ourselves on what only appears to be good for us. We cannot approach God without proper respect for His holiness.

Knowledge of the Divine. This is sanctifying oneself by abstaining from even that which is permitted. Such behavior brings to understanding.

Additional years of like. Years of prosperity and well-being.

Grow wise for yourself. The reward will belong to no one else but you.

The foolish woman chatters enticingly. Like the Torah, the evil inclination also calls out to people, but here the comparison ends. For the Torah calls out to people in an eloquent manner, and only once. In contrast, the evil inclination incessantly gives voice to its coarse enticements. This is a sure sign that it has nothing good to offer, for when someone wants to give away something good, he has no need to entice others to take it.

On a chair at the City's summit. In the manner of a prostitute, in contrast, the woman representing the Torah behaves modestly – she remains at home and sends her maidens to "call out upon the City's summit.

Who straightened their paths. Referring to individuals who have sinned, and who are in the process of straightening out their paths "through repentance." Stolen waters . . . bread eaten in secret . . both imply sin.

PROVERBS 10

1. The proverbs of Solomon. A wise son maketh a glad father: but a foolish son is the heaviness of his mother.

2. Treasures of wickedness profit nothing: but righteousness delivereth from death.

3. The Lord will not suffer the soul of the righteous to famish: but he casteth away the substance of the wicked.

4. He becometh poor that dealeth with a slack hand: but the hand of the diligent maketh rich.

5. He that gathereth in summer is a wise son: but he that sleepeth in harvest is a son that causeth shame.

6. Blessings are upon the head of the just: but violence covereth the mouth of the wicked.

7. The memory of the just is blessed: but the name of the wicked shall rot.

8. The wise in heart will receive commandments: but a prating fool shall fall.

9. He that walketh uprightly walketh surely: but he that perverteth his ways shall be known.

10. He that winketh with the eye causeth sorrow: but a prating fool shall fall.

11. The mouth of a righteous man is a well of life: but violence covereth the mouth of the wicked.

Gaining wealth should not become an end in itself. This effort does not provide the godly person reason to be lazy and not work. Wisdom leads to work by which we reap material security. Wisdom teaches us that work is important, but it calls us to use wise judgment in our work. It is most important to work when we can anticipate gaining the greatest results. One with integrity of purpose and character will live a life of openness before God and others. Those without such integrity must constantly work at keeping up a front wondering when they will be caught in their own trap of lies.

A wise son. . . A wise son spends his days in the study hall learning Torah alongside his Father, who derives great joy from hearing his son's wise words. But, a foolish son spends much of his time loafing at home in the presence of his mother, which saddens her to no end.

Riches . . . no avail. Wealth acquired through dishonest means will not save its owner on the day of judgment.

The deceitful hand . . . One who uses dishonest means to increase his profits will ultimately become a pauper, whereas one who is honest in all his business affairs will ultimately grow wealthy. The deceitful hand refers to those who "cheat" by circumventing study of the primary texts and, instead, study only the abridged code of law. The verse teaches that nothing is gained by this short-cut, for they will soon forget everything they learned.

Intelligent son. The verse alludes to Torah study; the springtime harvest represents one's youth, while the late summer reaping represents old age. An intelligent person continues studying Torah in old age, for although he can no longer absorb – "honest" – great amounts of new material, he can still progress in his studies by reviewing – "gathering" – the materials he learned in his youth. In contrast, the shameful son refrains from studying even in the prime of his life.

<u>Memory . . .</u> When the memory of a righteous person comes to mind, one fondly blesses the deceased. In contrast, when the memory of a wicked person comes to mind, the associations are as unpleasant as the odor of decomposing matter.

<u>The wise-hearted.</u> When the righteous are presented with the opportunity to fulfill one of God's commandments, they do so without delay. In contrast, the foolish talk much, but do little.

<u>The well-spring of life.</u> Torah is life. "Love" God your Lord, obey Him, and attach yourself to Him. This is your sole means of survival and long life (Deuteronomy 30:20). Therefore, when the righteous speak words of Torah they bring life to the entire world.

12. Hatred stirreth up strifes: but love covereth all sins.

13. In the lips of him that hath understanding wisdom is found: but a rod is for the back of him that is void of understanding.

14. Wise men lay up knowledge: but the mouth of the foolish is near destruction.

15. The rich man's wealth is his strong city: the destruction of the poor is their poverty.

16. The labour of the righteous tendeth to life: the fruit of the wicked to sin.

17. He is in the way of life that keepeth instruction: but he that refuseth reproof erreth.

18. He that hideth hatred with lying lips, and he that uttereth a slander, is a fool.

The work of love is to bring smoothness to relationships. Such love does not gloss over difficulties, rather, it provides the energy needed to bring the sometimes-difficult results of forgiveness and reconciliation. People are expected to develop their wisdom to its highest potential. Those who fail to do so can expect to suffer the consequences.

<u>Hatred stirs up quarrels.</u> When there is hatred between people, even the most insignificant fault can provoke a heated quarrel. When there is love between people, slight faults can be easily overlooked.

<u>Wisdom.</u> If a man of insight is rebuked, he rarely admits his mistakes, as did King David in the face of Nathan's reproof (II Samuel 12:13). Those without sense do not accept rebuke unless it is accompanied by punishment.

<u>Lying Lips.</u> In order to maintain his amicable facade, one who hides his hatred is forced to speak insincerely.

<u>One who speaks slander is a fool.</u> A slander causes himself harm, for people will quote to him the well-known truism: A fool sees his own faults in others.

19. In the multitude of words there wanteth not sin: but he that refraineth his lips is wise.

20. The tongue of the just is as choice silver: the heart of the wicked is little worth.

21. The lips of the righteous feed many: but fools die for want of wisdom.

22. The blessing of the Lord, it maketh rich, and he addeth no sorrow with it.

23. It is as sport to a fool to do mischief: but a man of understanding hath wisdom.

24. The fear of the wicked, it shall come upon him: but the desire of the righteous shall be granted.

25. As the whirlwind passeth, so is the wicked no more: but the righteous is an everlasting foundation.

26. As vinegar to the teeth, and as smoke to the eyes, so is the sluggard to them that send him.

27. The fear of the Lord prolongeth days: but the years of the wicked shall be shortened.

28. The hope of the righteous shall be gladness: but the expectation of the wicked shall perish.

The righteous man's tongue; which knows how to rebuke sinners.

Fleeting, some people do not repent for their sins, even after having listened to a righteous man's works of rebuke. This is not a reflection of the righteous man's shortcomings, for his tongue is "choice silver", but rather of the sinner's capriciousness. The righteous man's words always penetrate a sinner's heart, but unfortunately the effect is short-lived.

Provide sustenance for many. Many earn their livelihood as a direct consequence of a righteous individual's prayer and merits; providing guidance for many.

But fools die. Because they forsake the words of the righteous.

For the fool. It is as easy for a fool to plot evil, and for a man of discernment to exercise wisdom, as it is to laugh.

The lazy man. A metaphor for individuals who do not attempt to fulfill their personal mission in this world – rectifying their souls. Those who are in fellowship with God can look forward to joy, but those not in a right relationship with Him can look forward to nothing (Psalm 1:6).

29. The way of the Lord is strength to the upright: but destruction shall be to the workers of iniquity.

30. The righteous shall never be removed: but the wicked shall not inhabit the earth.

31. The mouth of the just bringeth forth wisdom: but the froward tongue shall be cut out.

32. The lips of the righteous know what is acceptable: but the mouth of the wicked speaketh frowardness.

<u>The righteous man.</u> After his death, he live on through his righteous descendants.

<u>The wicked will not inherit the earth.</u> They will have no descendants to carry on their lineage so, that in time, all memory of them will be erased.

<u>Know to appease</u> – God, and to make peace between people.

PROVERBS 11

1. A false balance is abomination to the LORD: but a just weight is his delight.

2. When pride cometh, then cometh shame: but with the lowly is wisdom.

3. The integrity of the upright shall guide them: but the perverseness of transgressors shall destroy them.

4. Riches profit not in the day of wrath: but righteousness delivereth from death.

5. The righteousness of the perfect shall direct his way: but the wicked shall fall by his own wickedness.

6. The righteousness of the upright shall deliver them: but transgressors shall be taken in their own naughtiness.

7. When a wicked man dieth, his expectation shall perish: and the hope of unjust men perisheth.

8. The righteous is delivered out of trouble, and the wicked cometh in his stead.

9. An hypocrite with his mouth destroyeth his neighbour: but through knowledge shall the just be delivered.

10. When it goeth well with the righteous, the city rejoiceth: and when the wicked perish, there is shouting.

Dishonesty is the opposite of the character traits God calls for and honors; justice, mercy, loving kindness and righteousness. If we use dishonesty to supply material needs, we need to ask God for wisdom to put life back in perspective. Wealth is not the final good; it carries potentially devastating power for character. It cannot satisfy the claim for righteousness demanded by God and fulfilled only through a faith relationship with Him. Wealth cannot purchase respect and good relationships in this life. Neither can it provide safety from God's judgement.

An "evil man" is one who studies God's word for the sole purpose of defeating others in argument; while "the humble" refers to a person who listens attentively to his teacher and overcomes the urge to interject his own opinions. The reward for humility is wisdom.

The Day of Wrath. When God punishes a sinner for his transgressions.

The innocent man's righteousness. "The innocent" refers to believers who have simple faith in God and do not rely at all on their intellectual capacities.

Hope is lost. The evil man's desires to rob the poor will remain unfulfilled all who placed their faith in the evil man will lose hope.

With a flattering mouth. An evil individual first gains the confidence of his victims through flattery, and therefore he proceeds to destroy them. "With a treacherous mouth . . . " he encourages others to commit transgressions; therefore, causing them to destroy themselves. He gives false testimony against others; he speaks slander against others.

11. By the blessing of the upright the city is exalted: but it is overthrown by the mouth of the wicked.

12. He that is void of wisdom despiseth his neighbour: but a man of understanding holdeth his peace.

13. A talebearer revealeth secrets: but he that is of a faithful spirit concealeth the matter.

14. Where no counsel is, the people fall: but in the multitude of counsellors there is safety.

15. He that is surety for a stranger shall smart for it: and he that hateth suretiship is sure.

16. A gracious woman retaineth honour: and strong men retain riches.

17. The merciful man doeth good to his own soul: but he that is cruel troubleth his own flesh.

18. The wicked worketh a deceitful work: but to him that soweth righteousness shall be a sure reward.

19. As righteousness tendeth to life: so he that pursueth evil pursueth it to his own death.

20. They that are of a froward heart are abomination to the Lord: but such as are upright in their way are his delight.

Loose treatment of the power of words can erode friendship.

A city rise. For a new city to prosper, it must have the blessings of the upright.

When there is no strategy. If in times of danger the Jewish people do not stop to reflect fast, and repent for their sins, then many of them will fall.

There is evil in store. The evil man will be destroyed for pledging . . .

Handshake – The handshake was a gesture for agreement concerning the terms of a financial contract.

<u>Illusory deeds</u> – The wicked mistakenly believes that their accomplishments will endure, when in fact, they are short-lived.

<u>True charity.</u> One who gives charity in good faith earns life, but if an evil man gives charity in order to deceive others into thinking he is righteous, then all he earns is death. From a physical perspective death is the normal end of human life.

<u>Men of treacherous hearts.</u> . . refers to individuals who harden their hearts and refuse to repent for their sins. They are an abomination to god. But if they should later have a change of heart and repent, God regards them as perfectly righteous.

21. Though hand join in hand, the wicked shall not be unpunished: but the seed of the righteous shall be delivered.

22. As a jewel of gold in a swine's snout, so is a fair woman which is without discretion.

23. The desire of the righteous is only good: but the expectation of the wicked is wrath.

24. There is that scattereth, and yet increaseth; and there is that withholdeth more than is meet, but it tendeth to poverty.

25. The liberal soul shall be made fat: and he that watereth shall be watered also himself.

26. He that withholdeth corn, the people shall curse him: but blessing shall be upon the head of him that selleth it.

<u>Hand to hand.</u> An idiomatic expression conveying that the punishment of the wicked will be administered by God's own "hand", and that it will not be revoked. The wicked will be punished in kind for their transgressions.

<u>A beautiful woman.</u> A metaphor for a Torah scholar who has gone astray. Instead of using his wisdom for Torah study, he utilizes it for sordid aims, such as to cheat and steal.

<u>Hope of the wicked is wrath.</u> They have no doubt that they will end up in Gehinnom because of their sins.

27. He that diligently seeketh good procureth favour: but he that seeketh mischief, it shall come unto him.

28. He that trusteth in his riches shall fall; but the righteous shall flourish as a branch.

29. He that troubleth his own house shall inherit the wind: and the fool shall be servant to the wise of heart.

30. The fruit of the righteous is a tree of life; and he that winneth souls is wise.

31. Behold, the righteous shall be recompensed in the earth: much more the wicked and the sinner.

<u>He who seeks good.</u> One tries to persuade others to walk in the way of the Torah.

<u>Pursues appeasement.</u> His ultimate goal is to improve the spiritual condition of the Jewish people to the point where God will be appeased by their deeds.

<u>He who trusts . . .</u> Some people regard their wealth as the most important thing in their lives. Consequently, if they would ever loose it, they would suffer emotional death. The righteous on the other hand regards wealth as though it were a leaf on a tree – the tree would shed its leaves in the fall, but it will surely bloom once again in spring.

<u>Destroys his household.</u> By remaining idle and not making an effort to earn a living.

The fool becomes a slave. The fool who "destroys" his household with his indolence will eventually need to sell himself as a slave in order to survive.

A tree of life. The reward which the righteous earns through their deeds is eternal, by teaching Torah to his children and disciples, a righteous person passes on to them "the Tree of Life", as in "keep my degrees and laws", since it is only by keeping them that a person can live. (Leviticus 18:5)

Acquires souls. That is, teaches Torah to others, as in the literal rendition of Genesis 12:5 – "Abram took his wife Sarai . . . as well as the souls that they had made. This refers to Abram's disciples.

If the righteous . . . King Solomon wonders how the wicked can ever feel secure. Is it not self-evident to them that if the righteous are punished for their transgressions during their lifetime, then certainly the same fate will befall them?

PROVERBS 12

1. Whoso loveth instruction loveth knowledge: but he that hateth reproof is brutish.

2. A good man obtaineth favour of the Lord: but a man of wicked devices will he condemn.

3. A man shall not be established by wickedness: but the root of the righteous shall not be moved.

4. A virtuous woman is a crown to her husband: but she that maketh ashamed is as rottenness in his bones.

5. The thoughts of the righteous are right: but the counsels of the wicked are deceit.

6. The words of the wicked are to lie in wait for blood: but the mouth of the upright shall deliver them.

7. The wicked are overthrown, and are not: but the house of the righteous shall stand.

8. A man shall be commended according to his wisdom: but he that is of a perverse heart shall be despised.

9. He that is despised, and hath a servant, is better than he that honoureth himself, and lacketh bread.

10. A righteous man regardeth the life of his beast: but the tender mercies of the wicked are cruel.

Parents must discipline children for children to have a change in life. Without discipline and correction, we never learn. Many verses in Proverbs stress the value of discipline in child guidance and point out the foolishness of resisting discipline.

Strong contrasts are made in Proverbs between wives who are acceptable in their behavior and those who are not. A good wife is valued as a gift from the Lord, but the bad wife is generally a quarrelsome one. A good wife is respected by her husband and brings honor to his name. Only a relationship of trust and commitment from both parties can lead to the respect and honor needed for family success.

<u>Love knowledge</u> – by accepting moral instruction, one accumulates new knowledge.

<u>Elicits God's favor</u>, and thereby brings blessings upon the world.

<u>He condemns . . .</u> A man's wickedness incites God to bring calamity upon the world, as in the verse, "one sinner destroys much good" (Ecclesiastes 9:18).

<u>The wicked . . .</u> When God looks upon the deeds of the wicked, they are doomed. Regarding the generation of the Flood, scripture states. "the Flood obliterated every organism that had been on the face of the earth." (Genesis 7:23); of the people of Sodom, it is written, "He overturned these cities . . . "; and of Egypt. The verse says, "Of all Pharoah's army that had followed (the Israelites) into the sea, not a single one remained (Exodus 14:28) .

<u>Corrupt at heart.</u> "A man of roaming heart" refers to someone who has abandoned the ways of the Torah; "a man with no ideas."

<u>Will be scorned.</u> Even if a person attempts to conceal his greatness from others by studying the Torah in absolute seclusion, word of his genius will

eventually filter out. Similarly, a wicked individual who attempts to hide his corruption from others will eventually be exposed.

It is better . . . It is preferable to toil and earn a living than to feel too noble for such a mental task. It is preferable to expose one's ignorance and ask questions rather than foreign comprehension and remain devoid of knowledge.

A righteous man . . . Because a righteous man is compassionate, he is aware of the needs of his entire household, including the lowliest beast. In contrast, the wicked are absolutely incapable of showing compassion – even when they appear to act compassionately, they are in truth - being cruel. Righteous people fulfill their physical needs but are careful not to overindulge.

11. He that tilleth his land shall be satisfied with bread: but he that followeth vain persons is void of understanding.

12. The wicked desireth the net of evil men: but the root of the righteous yieldeth fruit.

13. The wicked is snared by the transgression of his lips: but the just shall come out of trouble.

14. A man shall be satisfied with good by the fruit of his mouth: and the recompence of a man's hands shall be rendered unto him.

15. The way of a fool is right in his own eyes: but he that hearkeneth unto counsel is wise.

16. A fool's wrath is presently known: but a prudent man covereth shame.

17. He that speaketh truth sheweth forth righteousness: but a false witness deceit.

18. There is that speaketh like the piercings of a sword: but the tongue of the wise is health.

19. The lip of truth shall be established for ever: but a lying tongue is but for a moment.

20. Deceit is in the heart of them that imagine evil: but to the counsellors of peace is joy.

Consistent work, not idle dreaming of things past or future, brings necessary provisions for life planning is essential, but the majority of the time must be dedicated to work which achieves the plan.

Tills his land . . . Aside from the literal meaning of "tilling the land", it is a metaphor for reviewing one's Torah studies. The verse teaches that constant review is the only way to avoid forgetting the Torah knowledge one has accumulated.

Alternately, scripture prescribes how to attain the desired balance between studying Torah and working for a living: one should work as much as necessary in order to sustain one's body (til the land), but once this end has been achieved, one must devote the remainder of one's time to Torah study (have his fill of bread). The verse also teaches that a person who spends all his time working and does not set aside anytime at all for Torah study is devoid of sense, he pursues emptiness.

The hunt of evil. To rob and oppress the innocent and the righteous.

Transgressions of the lips. Such as were committed by the people of Noah's generation, who said, "Who is the almighty that we should serve him?"

Conceal his shame. The clever man spoken to in an abusive manner does not give expression to the humiliation he feels inside. He holds himself back from retaliating.

He who speaks. Only a person accustomed to always speaking the truth is capable of giving trustworthy testimony.

<u>Truthful speech.</u> True endures forever, but dishonesty is swiftly exposed. But, the lying tongue will be silent forever.

<u>Deceit . . . plot evil.</u> The fear of being discovered prevents them from ever feeling joy. Persons of integrity are marked by patience, slowness to anger, and humility. They are teachable.

21. There shall no evil happen to the just: but the wicked shall be filled with mischief.

22. Lying lips are abomination to the Lord: but they that deal truly are his delight.

23. A prudent man concealeth knowledge: but the heart of fools proclaimeth foolishness.

24. The hand of the diligent shall bear rule: but the slothful shall be under tribute.

25. Heaviness in the heart of man maketh it stoop: but a good word maketh it glad.

26. The righteous is more excellent than his neighbour: but the way of the wicked seduceth them.

27. The slothful man roasteth not that which he took in hunting: but the substance of a diligent man is precious.

28. In the way of righteousness is life: and in the pathway thereof there is no death.

Words can hurt or heal. Wise use of the power of words leads one to know the importance of timing, both knowing when to speak and when to listen.

<u>No iniquity will befall the righteous.</u> God will protect righteous individuals from unwillingly committing a transgression, or from even contemplating such a thing.

Lying lips. . . . refers to false witnesses, whereas those who behave honestly are judges who reject false testimony.

Conceals his knowledge. Due to his great humility, he is careful not to share his knowledge with unworthy individuals. Wisdom is self-evident and does not have to be advertised. People with little wisdom and much foolishness tend to talk more than the wise.

The diligent hand will rule. The upright will become wealthy. Those who work hard have an opportunity to achieve, while people who are lazy are most likely to lose even that which they have, including freedom.

Will not roast his gain. The wicked will not derive benefit from the wealth they acquire through deceitful means. Those who are in a right relationship with God are careful in their human relationships which they establish. Wrong human relationships can lead us away from God. We prize possessions for which we have worked because of the labor invested in them. However, patience must be exercised to achieve greater accomplishments. Long-term goals should not be sacrificed for short-term gain.

Human-Death – sin brings death and righteousness is the way of no death.

PROVERBS 13

1. A wise son heareth his father's instruction: but a scorner heareth not rebuke.

2. A man shall eat good by the fruit of his mouth: but the soul of the transgressors shall eat violence.

3. He that keepeth his mouth keepeth his life: but he that openeth wide his lips shall have destruction.

4. The soul of the sluggard desireth, and hath nothing: but the soul of the diligent shall be made fat.

5. A righteous man hateth lying: but a wicked man is loathsome, and cometh to shame.

6. Righteousness keepeth him that is upright in the way: but wickedness overthroweth the sinner.

7. There is that maketh himself rich, yet hath nothing: there is that maketh himself poor, yet hath great riches.

8. The ransom of a man's life are his riches: but the poor heareth not rebuke.

9. The light of the righteous rejoiceth: but the lamp of the wicked shall be put out.

10. Only by pride cometh contention: but with the well advised is wisdom.

<u>He who guards his mouth . . .</u> When a person succumbs to anger, the loftiest part of his soul temporarily abandons him. Desire, no matter how intense, will lead nowhere until people are willing to work for what they desire.

<u>Whose way is sincere.</u> That is, one who give charity with a pure heart and not for ulterior motives such as gaining fame.

<u>One becomes wealthy . . .</u> Those who become wealthy by robbing the poor will end up with nothing, but those who impoverish themselves by contributing generously to charity will earn great reward.

<u>A man's wealth . . . no reproof.</u> Charity atones for one's soul, as long as one does not embarrass the recipient. Wealth may pay the ransom when greedy persons threaten us. Righteous people without wealth do not have to endure such threats. What has wealth really purchased?

<u>The light . . .</u> "Light" represents the soul of the righteous, which will rejoice in the world to come. The wicked on the other hand, extinguishes the light of their own soul through their numerous transgressions. Light which the eyes see while people are living, is gone when death comes. Death follows upon sin. A wise person recognizes areas of personal ignorance and is willing to learn from others in such places. Pride robs us of the riches of others' knowledge, leading only to fights between friends.

11. Health gotten by vanity shall be diminished: but he that gathereth by labour shall increase.

12. Hope deferred maketh the heart sick: but when the desire cometh, it is a tree of life.

13. Whoso despiseth the word shall be destroyed: but he that feareth the commandment shall be rewarded.

14. The law of the wise is a fountain of life, to depart from the snares of death.

15. Good understanding giveth favour: but the way of transgressors is hard.

16. Every prudent man dealeth with knowledge: but a fool layeth open his folly.

17. A wicked messenger falleth into mischief: but a faithful ambassador is health.

18. Poverty and shame shall be to him that refuseth instruction: but he that regardeth reproof shall be honoured.

19. The desire accomplished is sweet to the soul: but it is abomination to fools to depart from evil.

20. He that walketh with wise men shall be wise: but a companion of fools shall be destroyed.

A fortune . . . A fortune earned through illicit means such as theft, will not endure, but one gathered through the soil of one's hands will increase: a person who does not exert his mind while studying may glean much knowledge, but he will soon forget it all. In contrast, one who soils in order to gain a deeper understanding may not cover much ground, but at least he will remember the little that he studied. If he persists, he will eventually become very wise.

He who scorns ... He who honors . . . Teaching originally denoted religious instruction in general, but later referred especially to the Law as it appears in the first five books of the Old Testament. Torah denotes both the process, and the content of instruction based on the Word of God. Therefore, the teaching activity of the wise cannot be separated from the substance of well-being to those who will listen. For this reason, Torah instructions in God's life-giving Word, will be an important aspect of the Messianic age.

A good mind wins favor. A person who has good intentions, good sense, wins the favor of God and man.

But the way of the treacherous is unbending. The wicked are so entrenched in their evil ways that even a man with a good mind who wins favor cannot convince them to change.

A healing. To the one who sent him. An example of a wicked messenger is Balaam (Numbers 22); an example of a faithful emissary is Moses.

Desire realized. When a person manages to realize his desire to heed reproof, his soul rejoices. We learn a great deal, both good and bad, by imitating the behavior of others.

21. Evil pursueth sinners: but to the righteous good shall be repayed.

22. A good man leaveth an inheritance to his children's children: and the wealth of the sinner is laid up for the just.

23. Much food is in the tillage of the poor: but there is that is destroyed for want of judgment.

24. He that spareth his rod hateth his son: but he that loveth him chasteneth him betimes.

25. The righteous eateth to the satisfying of his soul: but the belly of the wicked shall want.

Evil pursues . . . The punishment of the wicked is not dispensed by God, as in the verse, "Calamity does not emanate from the mouth of the Almighty." (Lamentations 3:38). Rather, their punishment is a natural consequence of their actions-the very evil they created through their sins becomes the force of retribution that inflicts them with their due measure of suffering.

Dr. Gilbert H. Edwards, Sr.

The wealth of a sinner . . . As the verse states, that very day King Ahasuerus gave the House of Haman, the enemy of the Jews, to Queen Esther . . . and Esther put Mordecai in charge of Haman's House (Esther 8:1-2).

Much food . . . In the past, the poor where the only ones willing to hire themselves, but for the back-breaking labor of cleaning a field of weeds and thorns. Only because of their toil did crops grow in abundance. Nevertheless, their wages were so measly that they could barely sustain themselves, and on occasion they actually died of starvation. Similarly, on the spiritual level, the world is blessed with abundance solely in the merit of the righteous – it is they who removed the spiritual "weeds and thorns" which prevent God's blessings from descending into the world.

He who spares his rod . . . A father who refrains from disciplining his young sone will later despise him when he becomes a delinquent. The one who is unwilling to discipline is itself an expression of hatred, for as a consequence of his father's misplaced compassion, the son will commit serious transgressions for which he will be sentenced to death.

PROVERBS 14

1. Every wise woman buildeth her house: but the foolish plucketh it down with her hands.

2. He that walketh in his uprightness feareth the LORD: but he that is perverse in his ways despiseth him.

3. In the mouth of the foolish is a rod of pride: but the lips of the wise shall preserve them.

4. Where no oxen are, the crib is clean: but much increase is by the strength of the ox.

5. A faithful witness will not lie: but a false witness will utter lies.

6. A scorner seeketh wisdom, and findeth it not: but knowledge is easy unto him that understandeth.

7. Go from the presence of a foolish man, when thou perceivest not in him the lips of knowledge.

8. The wisdom of the prudent is to understand his way: but the folly of fools is deceit.

9. Fools make a mock at sin: but among the righteous there is favour.

10. The heart knoweth his own bitterness; and a stranger doth not intermeddle with his joy.

Dr. Gilbert H. Edwards, Sr.

Wisdom put into action leads people to choose constructive ways of living and working. Foolishness self-destructs.

Where there are no oxen . . . The verse is to be understood metaphorically sound halakhic decisions cannot be formulated in a place where there are no Torah scholars. The proper use if the natural resources of the world offers the opportunity for prosperity for all.

Those seeking to development their wisdom and knowledge are willing to be open to the examination of themselves and others. This is the way of intellectual stimulation and growth.

The wisdom . . . is to understand his way. The basis of a clever man's wisdom is his ability to carefully consider his course of action in any given situation. The verse teaches that the primary function of a clever man's wisdom is to gain a better understanding of his own psyche, and thereby see through the crafty ploys of the evil inclination.

The foolishness of fools is deceit. The deceitful schemes that the wicked constantly turn over in their minds will cause them to become obtuse. Fools refer to people who do not stop to consider their course of action and, as a consequence, fall prey to the deceitful wiles of the evil inclination.

A guilt-admission. Because fools speak impetuously, they frequently6 need to apologize to those whom they have insulted. The righteous on the other hand, always choose their words carefully and so do not need to apologize to anyone for good-will always come in the wake of their words.

11. The house of the wicked shall be overthrown: but the tabernacle of the upright shall flourish.

12. There is a way which seemeth right unto a man, but the end thereof are the ways of death.

13. Even in laughter the heart is sorrowful; and the end of that mirth is heaviness.

14. The backslider in heart shall be filled with his own ways: and a good man shall be satisfied from himself.

15. The simple believeth every word: but the prudent man looketh well to his going.

16. A wise man feareth, and departeth from evil: but the fool rageth, and is confident.

17. He that is soon angry dealeth foolishly: and a man of wicked devices is hated.

18. The simple inherit folly: but the prudent are crowned with knowledge.

19. The evil bow before the good; and the wicked at the gates of the righteous.

20. The poor is hated even of his own neighbour: but the rich hath many friends.

There is a road . . . it leads to death. Initially, the smooth road of the wicked appears much more attractive than the road that leads to wisdom for the latter is full of obstacles that one must overcome. In the end however, the road of wickedness turns rocky and leads to death. While the rough road of the righteous becomes smooth and leads to life.

In the end, joy will sour. Scripture teaches that it is impossible to attain lasting joy in this temporal world.

A man whose heart withdraws from God. Eternal reward is likened to a tree: the wicked receive all of their reward – the leaves as well as the fruit – in the ephemeral currency of this world. The righteous on the other hand, receive only the leaves in this world, but the fruit is stored away for them to enjoy for all eternity in the world to come.

<u>Deliberates for his own benefit.</u> Deliberates [in order not to be swayed from] his course, understands the real point.

<u>A wise man fears God</u>; or punishment in the form of adversity; or temptation, unaided human nature leads people to make wrong choices leading ultimately to death. The untrained conscience cannot be a trusted guide. God has given people minds with the expectation that we will use them to evaluate everything we hear and see. We must decide for ourselves, not simply accept another's opinion blindly regardless of the position or education of the other person.

21. He that despiseth his neighbour sinneth: but he that hath mercy on the poor, happy is he.

22. Do they not err that devise evil? but mercy and truth shall be to them that devise good.

23. In all labour there is profit: but the talk of the lips tendeth only to penury.

24. The crown of the wise is their riches: but the foolishness of fools is folly.

25. A true witness delivereth souls: but a deceitful witness speaketh lies.

26. In the fear of the LORD is strong confidence: and his children shall have a place of refuge.

27. The fear of the LORD is a fountain of life, to depart from the snares of death.

Work does not necessarily produce financial profit immediately, but usually pays off in the long run. Empty words unaccompanied by work never produce profit of any kind. Talk, no matter how spiritual its application, must be backed by actions. Words without work lead to the spiritual poorhouse.

<u>The adornment of the wise is their wealth.</u> For material wealth, it fused properly, can help one attain greater wisdom. The verse teaches that it is desirable that the wise be wealthy so that common people not look down upon them.

<u>With the fear of God . . .</u> Referring to Abraham, to whom God said, "Now, I know that you fear God." (Genesis 22:12) Then God promised Abraham, "I have sworn by my own essence that . . . I will bless you greatly, and increase your offering like the stars of the sky and the sand on the seashore. Your offspring will inherit their enemies' gate.

28. In the multitude of people is the king's honour: but in the want of people is the destruction of the prince.

29. He that is slow to wrath is of great understanding: but he that is hasty of spirit exalteth folly.

30. A sound heart is the life of the flesh: but envy the rottenness of the bones.

31. He that oppresseth the poor reproacheth his Maker: but he that honoureth him hath mercy on the poor.

32. The wicked is driven away in his wickedness: but the righteous hath hope in his death.

33. Wisdom resteth in the heart of him that hath understanding: but that which is in the midst of fools is made known.

34. Righteousness exalteth a nation: but sin is a reproach to any people.

35. The king's favour is toward a wise servant: but his wrath is against him that causeth shame.

<u>A healing heart . . .</u> A heart that rectifiers evil by being tolerant towards others is a remedy for all mankind's character traits affect our physical health, as well as, our relationships with God and man. Quick temper,

envy, and oppression are foolish traits to cultivate. Patience is the opposite of quick temper. Peaceful hearts do not envy others, and kindness leaves no room for envy.

<u>One who robs . . . offends his maker.</u> For his actions are a manifestation of his belief that God is incapable of assisting helpless victims. Our loving response to persons in need pleases and honors God because He has shown Himself to be a God of grace and love, greatly concerned for person who are needy in distress. Poverty and human suffering are not adequate reasons for doubting the goodness of God the Creator. Human injustice is one major source of poverty. God constantly shows concern and compassion for the poor.

<u>A righteous man is secure.</u> (Isaiah 38:1-3) The righteous have God as their refuge even in death.

<u>Wisdom reposes. . .</u> Men of insight do not teach their wisdom to unworthy disciples. In contrast, the foolish share their shreds of wisdom with anyone who is willing to lend an ear. Even a person who is a fool can have access to the wisdom of God. God does not have secret knowledge; He wants to give only a few.

<u>Charity elevates a people . . .</u> "A people" refers specifically to Israel.- their charitable deeds elevate them in the eyes of God. On the other hand, the kindness of nations is regarded by God as sin, for their contributions so towards supporting idolatry.

PROVERBS 15

1. A soft answer turneth away wrath: but grievous words stir up anger.

2. The tongue of the wise useth knowledge aright: but the mouth of fools poureth out foolishness.

3. The eyes of the Lord are in every place, beholding the evil and the good.

4. A wholesome tongue is a tree of life: but perverseness therein is a breach in the spirit.

5. A fool despiseth his father's instruction: but he that regardeth reproof is prudent.

6. In the house of the righteous is much treasure: but in the revenues of the wicked is trouble.

7. The lips of the wise disperse knowledge: but the heart of the foolish doeth not so.

8. The sacrifice of the wicked is an abomination to the Lord: but the prayer of the upright is his delight.

9. The way of the wicked is an abomination unto the Lord: but he loveth him that followeth after righteousness.

10. Correction is grievous unto him that forsaketh the way: and he that hateth reproof shall die.

Language communicates our emotions and our intellect. In so doing, it attracts or repels people. Good communication is at the heart of good human relationships.

<u>The tree of life . . . for the tongue.</u> Torah study "The Tree of Life" Real tongues that have been stricken with sin of slander. Alternatively, "a healing tongue is a tree of life.," - "healing tongue" referring to moral instruction which lengthens the days of those who heed it.

<u>The house of the righteous . . .</u> A righteous man's moral values from a spiritual fortress that is impregnable to evil temptations. However, if such an individual makes the fatal mistake of incorporating into his belief system "the produce of wicked – values that conflict with the precept of the Torah – the ramparts of his mighty fortress has been seriously weakened. Sacrifice without righteousness is meaningless. It gains no favor without God. The prayers of the righteous pleases God.

<u>He who pursues righteousness will be loved.</u> He will be loved by God, even if he does not actually accomplish the righteous act that he set out to do. He who causes others to pursue righteousness will be loved. Those who choose righteousness over wickedness cn be assured of the presence and protection of God.

11. Hell and destruction are before the Lord: how much more then the hearts of the children of men?

12. A scorner loveth not one that reproveth him: neither will he go unto the wise.

13. A merry heart maketh a cheerful countenance: but by sorrow of the heart the spirit is broken.

14. The heart of him that hath understanding seeketh knowledge: but the mouth of fools feedeth on foolishness.

15. All the days of the afflicted are evil: but he that is of a merry heart hath a continual feast.

16. Better is little with the fear of the Lord than great treasure and trouble therewith.

17. Better is a dinner of herbs where love is, than a stalled ox and hatred therewith.

18. A wrathful man stirreth up strife: but he that is slow to anger appeaseth strife.

19. The way of the slothful man is as an hedge of thorns: but the way of the righteous is made plain.

20. A wise son maketh a glad father: but a foolish man despiseth his mother.

Breaks the spirit As well as one's motivation to achieve in both the material and spiritual realms, a hunger for knowledge is the mark of a wise person. Wisdom makes us understand our need for learning. The fool is a "know-it-all" satisfied in ignorance.

All the days . . . No matter how wealthy a person may be, if he covets the possessions of those wealthier than he is satisfied with his lot in life. Those who keep a sense of festival within their lives find their days more pleasant. People who dwell on their problems never know joy, God promises to reward His faithful servants, but rewards and wealth must not become our major concern in life. Possessing little and being faithful is greater than wealth without devotion to God.

Better a meal . . . It is preferable to serve a pauper a modest meal with affection than to feed him a lavish meal in an unfriendly manner.

The way of the lazy man . . . A lazy person always finds excuses to interrupt his endeavors, whereas the upright are never deterred by the obstacles they encounter. In connection with the lazy man, the word (way) appears, which conveys a wide road. However, in connection with the upright, the word (path) appears, which conveys a narrow trail. This teaches that the lazy find reasons to give up even under the best of conditions whereas the upright show a determination to persevere even when they encounter truly difficult situations.

21. Folly is joy to him that is destitute of wisdom: but a man of understanding walketh uprightly.

22. Without counsel purposes are disappointed: but in the multitude of counsellors they are established.

23. A man hath joy by the answer of his mouth: and a word spoken in due season, how good is it!

24. The way of life is above to the wise, that he may depart from hell beneath.

A man rejoices over his mouth's reply . . . The first clause emphasizes the importance of responding to people in a polite manner. A person who does so will surely benefit, for as a consequence of his soft-spoken replies, he will be well-liked by all. Those who are willing to work with others find better accomplishments through pooled wisdom.

The path of life . . . A person cannot stay on the same spiritual level for very long-unless he continues to advance ever upward, he will surely plumet and fall.

25. The Lord will destroy the house of the proud: but he will establish the border of the widow.

26. The thoughts of the wicked are an abomination to the Lord: but the words of the pure are pleasant words.

27. He that is greedy of gain troubleth his own house; but he that hateth gifts shall live.

28. The heart of the righteous studieth to answer: but the mouth of the wicked poureth out evil things.

29. The Lord is far from the wicked: but he heareth the prayer of the righteous.

30. The light of the eyes rejoiceth the heart: and a good report maketh the bones fat.

31. The ear that heareth the reproof of life abideth among the wise.

32. He that refuseth instruction despiseth his own soul: but he that heareth reproof getteth understanding.

33. The fear of the Lord is the instruction of wisdom; and before honour is humility.

By declaring what God is pleased and displeased with, the writer revealed the nature and will of God. He is God who rejects pride, supports weak, despises divided loyalties and blesses the individual heart.

Evil thoughts . . . God loathes individuals who speak with a pleasant demeaner while harboring evil intentions. Not only the deeds, but the very thoughts of people determine their relationship with God.

He who loathes gifts will live. A person who has complete faith in God and sincerely dislikes receiving anything from his fellow men, including gifts, will be given additional years of life – something which no human being could ever give him.

The heart . . . When asked for advice, a righteous man carefully weighs every alternative and exerts himself in thought. A wicked man, on the other hand, says the first thing that comes to his mind and has no record whatsoever for the welfare of the petitioner. The wicked alienates themselves. "Hears" implies that God will answer. He is faithful to His faithful people. The biblical writer repeatedly emphasized the relationship between learning and the quality of teachableness. Just as children can learn from parental discipline, so can we learn from constructive criticism all through life, if we have the humility to accept corrective advice.

PROVERBS 16

1. The preparations of the heart in man, and the answer of the tongue, is from the Lord.

2. All the ways of a man are clean in his own eyes; but the Lord weigheth the spirits.

3. Commit thy works unto the Lord, and thy thoughts shall be established.

4. The Lord hath made all things for himself: yea, even the wicked for the day of evil.

5. Every one that is proud in heart is an abomination to the Lord: though hand join in hand, he shall not be unpunished.

6. By mercy and truth iniquity is purged: and by the fear of the Lord men depart from evil.

7. When a man's ways please the Lord, he maketh even his enemies to be at peace with him.

8. Better is a little with righteousness than great revenues without right.

9. A man's heart deviseth his way: but the Lord directeth his steps.

10. A divine sentence is in the lips of the king: his mouth transgresseth not in judgment.

The designs . . . Man was given complete control over his thoughts, but the words by which he expresses himself are determined by God. If a person should ever be required to address someone important, he would benefit more from focusing his heart on God than from mentally rehearsing his speech. The same principle applies to Torah study when a person diligently applies himself to understanding the Torah, God grants him the intellectual faculties required to achieve this goal.

. . . for the day of evil . . . God grants power to the wicked so that they might commit additional transgressions and consequently render themselves deserving of the Torah punishment that awaits them on the day of judgement.

Completely turns away from evil. Better than atoning for one's sins is not to have sinned at all. Fear of God is even more valuable than kindness and truth.

When God is pleased . . . This refers back to the previous verse which call on the wicked to repent for their sins through "kindness and truth." There are three obstacles or "enemies" that a penitent must overcome: His evil inclination, the influences of his environment and his earthly desires. Our verse teaches that although these obstacles may seem insurmountable, there is no reason to fear them – when God is pleased by a penitent's efforts to repent for his sins. He will cause his three "enemies" to make peace with him. Following God's revealed purpose is the only effective way to conduct life. We are free to choose as we will, but God takes every event and works His own will into it. He is active in each event to produce His own purposes. Thus, God's gift of individual freedom is balanced by His fidelity to His own purposes. He will work in every situation to save and redeem in accordance with His will.

A man's heart . . . A person merely has to think of repenting for his sins and God immediately assists him by guiding him towards the proper path. "One who comes to purify himself is assisted."

11. A just weight and balance are the Lord's: all the weights of the bag are his work.

12. It is an abomination to kings to commit wickedness: for the throne is established by righteousness.

13. Righteous lips are the delight of kings; and they love him that speaketh right.

14. The wrath of a king is as messengers of death: but a wise man will pacify it.

15. In the light of the king's countenance is life; and his favour is as a cloud of the latter rain.

16. How much better is it to get wisdom than gold! and to get understanding rather to be chosen than silver!

17. The highway of the upright is to depart from evil: he that keepeth his way preserveth his soul.

18. Pride goeth before destruction, and an haughty spirit before a fall.

19. Better it is to be of an humble spirit with the lowly, than to divide the spoil with the proud.

20. He that handleth a matter wisely shall find good: and whoso trusteth in the Lord, happy is he.

<u>Shining countenance.</u> Alluding to the Torah – one who studies it is granted life, as in "she is a tree of life for those who hold on to her."

<u>His favor . . .</u> This alludes to the favor won from God through prayer and the fulfillment of Mitzvoth. Scripture teaches that in the next world, a person will first receive the reward he earned by studying Torah ("life"), and only afterwards the reward for having prayed and performed Mitzvoth.

<u>Preceding ruin there is power. . .</u> God increases the authority of the wicked shortly before bringing about their demise. Their short lived power makes them arrogant, and so deserving of intensified suffering wisdom is a far

more lasting attainment than wealth. Pride and humility contrasted in this Proverb provide some insight into the overarching biblical perspective that pride is a negative virtue while humility is to be cultivated.

<u>He who considers . . . trust in God.</u> If a person makes a great effort to understand the Torah, he is guaranteed to succeed. The same cannot be said of material endeavors. Even if one makes a great effort to earn a livelihood, he will not necessarily succeed. In such matters, the only guarantee for success is complete trust in God.

21. The wise in heart shall be called prudent: and the sweetness of the lips increaseth learning.

22. Understanding is a wellspring of life unto him that hath it: but the instruction of fools is folly.

23. The heart of the wise teacheth his mouth, and addeth learning to his lips.

24. Pleasant words are as an honeycomb, sweet to the soul, and health to the bones.

25. There is a way that seemeth right unto a man, but the end thereof are the ways of death.

26. He that laboureth laboureth for himself; for his mouth craveth it of him.

27. An ungodly man diggeth up evil: and in his lips there is as a burning fire.

28. A froward man soweth strife: and a whisperer separateth chief friends.

<u>A man of insight.</u> A disciple who grows wise from the lessons of his master will eventually develop the ability to infer one idea from another, and thus will be called "a man of insight."

<u>A man of pleasing words gains erudition.</u> Someone who explains his teachings to others is rewarded two-fold; in addition to the reward he earns for enabling others to understand, he himself gains a deeper comprehension of the material.

<u>Pleasant sayings.</u> Words of Torah.

<u>The soul . . . the bones.</u> A person who studies Torah during his lifetime will be spared the pain that the body and soul feels inside the grave.

<u>Will the soul . . .</u> It is pure folly for a man to sacrifice the pursuit of spiritual growth for the sake of fulfilling his physical desires. If nothing else motivates, physical need should drive people to diligent work.

<u>A godless man.</u> "A man with no yoke."

<u>A scorching fire is on his lips.</u> Referring to his evil schemes or to his infuriating manner of speech.

<u>A wily man.</u> Referring to someone wo distorts the words of others in order to instigate quarrels between people. Who persuades others to follow his example and commit transgressions.

<u>A complainer.</u> "An inciter" wo spreads false rumors.

<u>Alienates a leader.</u> His complaints against the leader of a nation causes that leader to become alienated from the people.

29. A violent man enticeth his neighbour, and leadeth him into the way that is not good.

30. He shutteth his eyes to devise froward things: moving his lips he bringeth evil to pass.

31. The hoary head is a crown of glory, if it be found in the way of righteousness.

32. He that is slow to anger is better than the mighty; and he that ruleth his spirit than he that taketh a city.

33. The lot is cast into the lap; but the whole disposing thereof is of the Lord.

<u>Attained by way of righteousness.</u> For righteousness adds years to one's life.

<u>Better is a man . . .</u> A warrior can vanquish only those weaker than himself, whereas a man of forbearance can overcome all. There is a subtle difference between a warrior and the conqueror of a city; the warrior requires nothing but brute strength, for his only goal is to destroy his adversary. The conqueror also requires planning and ingenuity, for although his soul is to capture the city, it is in his best interest to cause the least possible damage during the battle. This is why the verse compares "a man of forbearance" with a warrior – forbearance requires only strength, for in order to attain it, one must completely subdue one's anger. "A master over his spirit", is compared to the conqueror of a city, for one should not completely subdue one's physical desires, but rather re-channel them into the service of God.

<u>A lot is cast . . . from God.</u> Casting of lots does not determine one's fate, for that is something that only God can do. Age does not bring wisdom automatically. One who has sought the life of righteousness will reflect that righteousness in old age. Respect and praise will crown the life of the righteous elderly. God controls the lots – probably specially marked stones – used in determining God's will.

PROVERBS 17

1. Better is a dry morsel, and quietness therewith, than a house full of sacrifices with strife.

2. A wise servant shall have rule over a son that causeth shame, and shall have part of the inheritance among the brethren.

3. The fining pot is for silver, and the furnace for gold: but the LORD trieth the hearts.

4. A wicked doer giveth heed to false lips; and a liar giveth ear to a naughty tongue.

5. Whoso mocketh the poor reproacheth his Maker: and he that is glad at calamities shall not be unpunished.

6. Children's children are the crown of old men; and the glory of children are their fathers.

7. Excellent speech becometh not a fool: much less do lying lips a prince.

8. A gift is as a precious stone in the eyes of him that hath it: whithersoever it turneth, it prospereth.

9. He that covereth a transgression seeketh love; but he that repeateth a matter separateth very friends.

10. A reproof entereth more into a wise man than an hundred stripes into a fool.

Better dry bread . . . Verse one explains why God destroyed the temple. He needed a respite from the Israelites endless transgressions.

Slave . . . Son . . . brothers. Verse two alludes to three types of righteous individuals listed here in ascending order: the "slave" represents those who devote their time to prayer, and the fulfilling of Mitzvoth; the "son" represents those who study the Torah; the "brothers" are those who ponder the esoteric teachings of the Torah. The verse teaches that a sincere "slave" is greater than a "son" with impure motives, and that such a "slave" will eventually reach the level of a "brother."

God for testing the heart. The purity of metals can be determined by heating them in a crucible or a furnace, but the purity of a man's heart can only be ascertained by God. The company we keep feeds our tongue. We will communicate to others what we listen to. Eventually, we usually believe and become what we constantly hear.

Offends his maker. By mocking the pauper, he insinuates that a person's natural abilities determine whether he will be rich poor, when in fact, it is God who determines the fate of every individual. God is concerned for persons who suffer in any way.

It enlightens him. A bride "enlightens" the recipient, so to speak, for now he suddenly sees how to interpret even damning evidence as, clearly substantiating the case of the one who proffered him that bribe. The verse warns against offering a bribe to a fellow Jew. (Leviticus 16:8)

He who overlooks . . . When one person commits an injustice against another, the injured party tends to perpetually spite the aggressor and never lets him forget his sin. If the injured party would overlook the injustice and act as though nothing had happened, he would earn the love and respect of the aggressor.

He who belabors a matter . . . A person who continuously recounts an injustice committed against him alienates God "the leader", as scripture states: "Do not take revenge or bear a grudge against the children of your people." (Leviticus 19:18) A right understanding of love will issue in forgiveness and forgetfulness about an offensive act.

11. An evil man seeketh only rebellion: therefore a cruel messenger shall be sent against him.

12. Let a bear robbed of her whelps meet a man, rather than a fool in his folly.

13. Whoso rewardeth evil for good, evil shall not depart from his house.

14. The beginning of strife is as when one letteth out water: therefore leave off contention, before it be meddled with.

15. He that justifieth the wicked, and he that condemneth the just, even they both are abomination to the LORD.

16. Wherefore is there a price in the hand of a fool to get wisdom, seeing he hath no heart to it?

17. A friend loveth at all times, and a brother is born for adversity.

18. A man void of understanding striketh hands, and becometh surety in the presence of his friend.

19. He loveth transgression that loveth strife: and he that exalteth his gate seeketh destruction.

20. He that hath a froward heart findeth no good: and he that hath a perverse tongue falleth into mischief.

Perverse tongue falleth into mischief.

Invites evil . . . against him. He invites evil in this world, and a cruel angel will be sent to punish him in the world to come.

Better than a man encounter . . . It is better to come face to face with a ferocious bear than with a fool who tries to convince one to forsake God.

Let's loose the floodgates. One who initiates a quarrel makes a hole in a dam (figuratively speaking), and in time, the hole grows progressively wider.

Before it comes out into the open. That is before it picks up momentum, at which point you will no longer be able to abandon it.

What is the price of wisdom doing . . . Why does the fool pay people to teach him Torah if deep in his heart he has no intention of ever fulfilling the commandments, or if his mind is incapable of grasping its subtle concepts, or if in his heart he does not desire to learn?

One loves a friend . . . but a brother . . . A person always loves his friend, but he expressed love for his brother only when misfortune occurs. Genuine friends love one another regardless of the situations which they face. People especially need to sustain both friends and family in times of adversity. Character is shown by our ability to form friendships. Friends never desert or ignore you. In life's toughest times, friends find ways to help.

Speaks haughtily. Raises his voice and speaks haughtily with his mouth. He "invites ruin."

21. He that begetteth a fool doeth it to his sorrow: and the father of a fool hath no joy.

22. A merry heart doeth good like a medicine: but a broken spirit drieth the bones.

23. A wicked man taketh a gift out of the bosom to pervert the ways of judgment.

24. Wisdom is before him that hath understanding; but the eyes of a fool are in the ends of the earth.

25. A foolish son is a grief to his father, and bitterness to her that bare him.

26. Also to punish the just is not good, nor to strike princes for equity.

27. He that hath knowledge spareth his words: and a man of understanding is of an excellent spirit.

28. Even a fool, when he holdeth his peace, is counted wise: and he that shutteth his lips is esteemed a man of understanding.

<u>One begets a fool . . .</u> The verse refers to someone who teaches Torah to an unworthy Christian. Such a Christian will invariably cause his teacher great sorrow. Therefore, the teacher is said to have given birth to his own sorrow. Our outlook on life has a significant effect on our physical well-being.

<u>From the bosom.</u> He takes the bribe stealthily in order to avoid being discovered.

<u>Wisdom is right in front. . . .</u> A fool despairs of ever attaining wisdom. For he thinks "How will I ever learn the entire Torah?" A man with understanding sees it as an easy task, for he thinks to himself, "I will learn two chapters a day and in time, I will know the entire Torah", or the verse teaches that a man of understanding is willing to learn Torah from local scholars who are "in front of him". A fool considers it beneath his dignity to learn from local scholars whom he deems second-rate. Therefore, he sets his sights on traveling to the other end of the world, where he will study from "truly great scholars.

<u>A foolish son angers . . . embitters . . .</u> The behavior of children affects their parents. The very nature of parenting is to suffer for the problems of the children.

<u>He who is not good. . . .</u> A wicked man detests righteousness to such a degree that he cannot retain himself from punishing righteous individuals with undue harshness. As far as he is concerned, their righteousness is pure evil. Words expose a person's ignorance quicker than silence.

PROVERBS 18

1. Through desire a man, having separated himself, seeketh and intermeddleth with all wisdom.

2. A fool hath no delight in understanding, but that his heart may discover itself.

3. When the wicked cometh, then cometh also contempt, and with ignominy reproach.

4. The words of a man's mouth are as deep waters, and the wellspring of wisdom as a flowing brook.

5. It is not good to accept the person of the wicked, to overthrow the righteous in judgment.

6. A fool's lips enter into contention, and his mouth calleth for strokes.

7. A fool's mouth is his destruction, and his lips are the snare of his soul.

8. The words of a talebearer are as wounds, and they go down into the innermost parts of the belly.

9. He also that is slothful in his work is brother to him that is a great waster.

10. The name of the LORD is a strong tower: the righteous runneth into it, and is safe.

Detaches himself from God. Pursues desire, or "He who detaches himself will pursue desire." By following the ways of Torah, a person learns to control his physical desires. Therefore, when someone forsakes the Torah he naturally regresses to man's lesser states in which succumbing to the body's desires is regarded as a matter of course. The Hebrew term for "unfriendly" describes a person who separates from others. Those who do so are depriving both themselves and others of the benefits of working together. Such an approach to life is foolish.

To disclose what is in his heart. To air his foolish thoughts or, to teach others the little wisdom in his possession. Poor communication destroys relationships.

The words of a man. . . A wise man's words are as pure as deep waters and as everlasting as a flowing stream.

The lips . . . Through his belligerent manner of speech, he acquires enemies who seek to cause him harm, or the harsh punishment incurred by someone who speaks slander.

To the depths of one's insides. While physical blows harm the body, being the victim of false rumors causes injury to one's soul. Also, injuries caused by physical blows eventually heal, but the effects of verbal jabs are irreversible.

Even he who . . . A sage who forsakes the Torah is a brother to satan, or the verse teaches that a sage who fails to study diligently will eventually adopt the heretical views of apostates who disgrace the Torah with their revisionist theories.

In evaluating the importance of work, those who destroy are seen to be of the same type as those who do not work with diligence.

11. The rich man's wealth is his strong city, and as an high wall in his own conceit.

12. Before destruction the heart of man is haughty, and before honour is humility.

13. He that answereth a matter before he heareth it, it is folly and shame unto him.

14. The spirit of a man will sustain his infirmity; but a wounded spirit who can bear?

15. The heart of the prudent getteth knowledge; and the ear of the wise seeketh knowledge.

16. A man's gift maketh room for him, and bringeth him before great men.

17. He that is first in his own cause seemeth just; but his neighbour cometh and searcheth him.

18. The lot causeth contentions to cease, and partly between the mighty.

The rich man's wealth . . . In its effort to dissuade people from serving God, the evil inclination wages war from every direction. It cloaks itself in the guise of society, which ridicules the God-fearing and labels them abnormal for having diverged from the accepted norms. Simultaneously, it enters one's consciousness and foments self-doubt. The verse teaches that a person's wealth-the Torah-protects him from the dangers which lurk within and without. We must know the question before we can give an answer. Otherwise, we appear foolish.

Acquires knowledge . . . seek knowledge. A person endowed with insight is capable of acquiring knowledge independently. Even the wise has no choice but to obtain knowledge from others.

A man's gift . . . This verse teaches that one who gives generously to charity is rewarded twofold: he receives a great portion in the world to come and also rises in esteem in this world. (Deuteronomy 12:19).

<u>The first . . .</u> The verse alludes to the interplay between the positive and negative forces in man; because, the evil inclination enters a person's being the moment he is born, he is more apt to follow its counsel over that of the good. Inclination which comes at a much later stage in life.

19. A brother offended is harder to be won than a strong city: and their contentions are like the bars of a castle.

20. A man's belly shall be satisfied with the fruit of his mouth; and with the increase of his lips shall he be filled.

21. Death and life are in the power of the tongue: and they that love it shall eat the fruit thereof.

22. Whoso findeth a wife findeth a good thing, and obtaineth favour of the LORD.

23. The poor useth intreaties; but the rich answereth roughly.

24. A man that hath friends must shew himself friendly: and there is a friend that sticketh closer than a brother.

<u>A wronged brother . . .</u> An individual wronged by his brother will still not turn him away in his time of need. This is because a quarrel between brothers is never permanent. Destroyed relationships create barriers between people. God's word calls us to maintain good relationships with others.

<u>Death and life . . .</u> One who speaks slander will die, whereas one who speaks words of Torah will live. The power of the tongue to sway is awesome. One who realizes that and uses the tongue rightly will enjoy a rich, meaningful life. Our use of language should be productive, helping us reach our goals.

<u>He who finds a wife . . .</u> He has found good because his wife will help him with his work, and he has won the favor of God because she will keep him from sinning.

<u>Friends . . . a brother.</u> A man makes friends so that he will appear friendly, but a single loved one is closes thana brother. Someone who surrounds himself with many friends is really alone, whereas a close and trusted friend is eve more beloved than a brother. People need the strength of a few solid relationships rather than a large number of superficial ones which offer no support.

PROVERBS 19

1. Better is the poor that walketh in his integrity, than he that is perverse in his lips, and is a fool.

2. Also, that the soul be without knowledge, it is not good; and he that hasteth with his feet sinneth.

3. The foolishness of man perverteth his way: and his heart fretteth against the Lord.

4. Wealth maketh many friends; but the poor is separated from his neighbour.

5. A false witness shall not be unpunished, and he that speaketh lies shall not escape.

6. Many will intreat the favour of the prince: and every man is a friend to him that giveth gifts.

7. All the brethren of the poor do hate him: how much more do his friends go far from him? he pursueth them with words, yet they are wanting to him.

8. He that getteth wisdom loveth his own soul: he that keepeth understanding shall find good.

9. A false witness shall not be unpunished, and he that speaketh lies shall perish.

10. Delight is not seemly for a fool; much less for a servant to have rule over princes.

Better a pauper . . . It is preferable to earn a modest living through hones means than to earn a fortune through deceit. A person who chooses the latter option is a fool, for he will not succeed.

He who pushes . . . sins. A person who impulsively pursues the desires of his heart is regarded as a sinner. For one must first stop to consider whether one's actions will bring one to sin. The verse warns against pretending to be more pious than one really is, for one who does so will surely stumble and fall.

Parts from his companion, or his companion parts from him.

His alone. Even the poor man's casual conversation with his relatives and friends fall on deaf ears. His words are his alone.

A heart. The quality of understanding.

Pleasure is not fitting . . . Pleasure is harmful to a fool because as long as he is savoring it, he will not change his ways. Power does not befit a slave because his subjects are liable to emulate his lowly traits.

11. The discretion of a man deferreth his anger; and it is his glory to pass over a transgression.

12. The king's wrath is as the roaring of a lion; but his favour is as dew upon the grass.

13. A foolish son is the calamity of his father: and the contentions of a wife are a continual dropping.

14. House and riches are the inheritance of fathers: and a prudent wife is from the Lord.

15. Slothfulness casteth into a deep sleep; and an idle soul shall suffer hunger.

16. He that keepeth the commandment keepeth his own soul; but he that despiseth his ways shall die.

17. He that hath pity upon the poor lendeth unto the Lord; and that which he hath given will he pay him again.

18. Chasten thy son while there is hope, and let not thy soul spare for his crying.

<u>An intelligent man is forbearing.</u> This is the inverse of a "short-tempered person commits folly."

<u>The wrath of a King . . .</u> Here "King" is an allusion to God. When His wrath is unleashed, even those who are not afflicted tremble with fear as though from the roar of a lion. On the other hand, the favor will show the righteous when He will revive the dead is likened to the beneficial effect of dew upon grass, as it is written, "Men will sprout up from the city of grass of the field." (Psalm72:16)

The maintenance of family relationships is the responsibility of each member of the family. Bad family relationships destroy its members.

<u>"Shiftiness"</u> Carries the idea of idleness. The opposite of being involved in work.

<u>Is negligent of his ways.</u> "Scorns his ways" by refraining to take stock of his deeds.

<u>He who shows mercy . . .</u> The verse emphasizes that money given to charity is never given, since God will surely reimburse it. Rather one should regard a gift of charity as a temporary loan to God. God makes a loan to the one who shows mercy to the poor.

He will pay him his reward. A person who gives charity will not only be reimbursed but will also be rewarded for his generosity.

Discipline your son. . . Even is your efforts to discipline your child do not seem to be bearing fruit, do not be dissuaded. There is still hope that if you persist, your message will eventually seep in. However, under no circumstances may you even consider putting an end to him because of his wickedness. The verse stresses that while spanking may be a valuable educational took, it must be used sparingly.

Parents can spare their children grief later in life is they will correct and guide them in their younger years. The Hebrew Yasser means both discipline or rebuke and teach or guide. Parent's discipline should always be corrective in nature, never vindictive. Parenthood can contribute to trouble and unhappiness in the lives of children, and sometimes even to their deaths.

19. A man of great wrath shall suffer punishment: for if thou deliver him, yet thou must do it again.

20. Hear counsel, and receive instruction, that thou mayest be wise in thy latter end.

21. There are many devices in a man's heart; nevertheless the counsel of the Lord, that shall stand.

22. The desire of a man is his kindness: and a poor man is better than a liar.

23. The fear of the Lord tendeth to life: and he that hath it shall abide satisfied; he shall not be visited with evil.

24. A slothful man hideth his hand in his bosom, and will not so much as bring it to his mouth again.

25. Smite a scorner, and the simple will beware: and reprove one that hath understanding, and he will understand knowledge.

26. He that wasteth his father, and chaseth away his mother, is a son that causeth shame, and bringeth reproach.

27. Cease, my son, to hear the instruction that causeth to err from the words of knowledge.

28. An ungodly witness scorneth judgment: and the mouth of the wicked devoureth iniquity.

29. Judgments are prepared for scorners, and stripes for the back of fools.

An ingredient of wisdom is the recognition of personal intellectual needs combined with the ability to accept and utilize education.

<u>Many are the thoughts . . .</u> People consider endless possibilities for how best to perform a task, carefully weighing the pros and cons of each. In the end, they will follow whichever plan God instills into their hearts.

<u>A man's appeal. . .</u> A sure way to become popular is to promise great rewards to many people. However, an individual who makes promises but does not keep his word is worse than a pauper, for at least the pauper does not raise false expectations.

<u>Strike the scoffer . . .</u> Mere rebuke does not motivate a scoffer to repent. Only when struck with calamity does he reason that he had better change his ways.\

Conversely a naïve person (one who consistently falls prey to the enticements of the evil inclinations) doe not even need to be rebuked, for merely learning of the adversity that befell the scoffer will make him realize that it is to his advance to repent. There is only one type of person upon whom rebuke works – someone who is discerning.

<u>A shameful and humiliating son . . .</u> A son who brings shame to his father strains the relationship between his parents, for the father will attribute his son's faults to the inadequate education provided by the mother. As a

result, the parents will divorce, and the father will have to pay large sums of money towards the mother's alimony. Therefore, this son effectively "robs his father and chases away his mother."

Moral instruction . . . Referring to the teachings of heretics posing as God-fearing preachers. They gain the confidence of their audience by starting off their lectures with words of reproof, and then expounding their poisonous ideas.

Speakes eloquently of justice. In order to convince the judge that he is telling the truth, alternatively, the verse refers to heretics who lead people astray by teaching them that certain Torah laws are no longer relevant, or that they are not meant to be taken literally.

Swallow iniquity. "Swallow" suggests to conceal or cloak, as in Numbers 4:20. The wicked conceal their iniquitous beliefs within the Torah lessons in order to instill ideas into their victims' minds subliminally, or the verse teaches that the wicked deny outright that their evil deeds constitute transgressions.

Punishments are in store for the scoffers. God said, "Before I created man, I prepared ways to afflict him, for I knew his true nature; as it is written, 'the inclination of man's heart' is evil from his youth (Genesis 8:21).

PROVERBS 20

1. Wine is a mocker, strong drink is raging: and whosoever is deceived thereby is not wise.

2. The fear of a king is as the roaring of a lion: whoso provoketh him to anger sinneth against his own soul.

3. It is an honour for a man to cease from strife: but every fool will be meddling.

4. The sluggard will not plow by reason of the cold; therefore shall he beg in harvest, and have nothing.

5. Counsel in the heart of man is like deep water; but a man of understanding will draw it out.

6. Most men will proclaim every one his own goodness: but a faithful man who can find?

7. The just man walketh in his integrity: his children are blessed after him.

8. A king that sitteth in the throne of judgment scattereth away all evil with his eyes.

9. Who can say, I have made my heart clean, I am pure from my sin?

Dr. Gilbert H. Edwards, Sr.

10. Divers weights, and divers measures, both of them are alike abomination to the Lord.

The wine-babbling scoffers . . . "Wine makes one scoffer, strong drink makes one boisterous."

Misled by it. Although a little liquor stimulates one's perceptiveness, do not be misled into thinking that much drink makes one wise; or it refers to frivolity. The words of the Torah are liken to oil. Just as oil floats away when a little water is added, so does Torah knowledge, disappears when accompanied by even a little frivolity.

Verse one is part of the lengthy chain of thought stretching from Genesis 9:21 to Isaiah 5:11-12; and beyond which expresses consciousness of ted aners inherent in wine. Wise people do not give alcoholic drinks the opportunity to control their minds and take away their wisdom. They do not want to become silly braggarts and stupid brawlers.

Every fool is exposed. Letting his temper flare exposes his foolishness to all. Every food becomes embroiled.

Insight draws it out. An insightful student is capable of extracting the wisdom in his teacher's mind; by inferring one thought from another.

With the majority . . . Many people boast about how kind they are, but for the most part greatly exaggerate. The verse questions whether there exist a man who tells only the truth about himself. Many people call out to friends but who can find a man who will keep his word?

The King. God judging the world; or a corporeal judge sincerely interested in passing a true verdict.

Who can say . . . Since it is impossible for man to completely avoid sin; or, the verse questions how anyone dares to deny his guilt before God. Since as in verse 8, everything is revealed before Him.

102

<u>Two different weights</u> . . . As in Deuteronomy 25:13-16.

11. Even a child is known by his doings, whether his work be pure, and whether it be right.

12. The hearing ear, and the seeing eye, the Lord hath made even both of them.

13. Love not sleep, lest thou come to poverty; open thine eyes, and thou shalt be satisfied with bread.

14. It is naught, it is naught, saith the buyer: but when he is gone his way, then he boasteth.

15. There is gold, and a multitude of rubies: but the lips of knowledge are a precious jewel.

16. Take his garment that is surety for a stranger: and take a pledge of him for a strange woman.

17. Bread of deceit is sweet to a man; but afterwards his mouth shall be filled with gravel.

18. Every purpose is established by counsel: and with good advice make war.

19. He that goeth about as a talebearer revealeth secrets: therefore meddle not with him that flattereth with his lips.

<u>Even in his deeds</u> . . . In general, a younger's deeds are regarded as brash and foolish. However, even he can change his image by refraining from sin and acting in an upright manner.

<u>God made both of them.</u> The ear in order to enable man to hear rebuke, and eye that may foresee what lies in store for him.

Human ability to perceive and understand God has much to do with our alertness and openness. To see an hear God is a question of being aware and seeking what God wishes to communicate.

The buyer . . This is the old age pattern of business transactions: the customer points out the faults of the merchandise in order to cajole the seller to lower the price. If successful, he walks away happy with his purchase and congratulates himself for his bargaining expertise. This is a metaphor for one who studies Torah in poverty. At first, he complains over his miserable condition. However, when he finally attains wisdom, he congratulates himself for having endured such discomfort. For the eternal reward one receives for studying Torah is commensurate to the difficulties experienced in the process.

Language can be used to secure goods through proper bargaining procedures. One expects, particularly in near Eastern bargaining to down grade the quality of goods being offered until the sale is final. Then the buyer claims to have gotten the best of the deal. Material wealth is not the highest value of life. Lips devoted to wisdom rank high on the priority scale and low on the availability scale.

Take his garment . . . Th subject of the verse if a person who embraces external ideologies in place of Torah, figuratively "pledging security" for them. The male stranger represents false philosophies, the foreign woman is idolatrous beliefs. One who supports such false ideologies will be stripped of the "spiritual garment" which every Jew received at Mount Sinai.

Wage ware with stratagems. If you decide to wage war against Satan, do it with effective stratagems – repent for your sins, pray and fast.

20. Whoso curseth his father or his mother, his lamp shall be put out in obscure darkness.

21. An inheritance may be gotten hastily at the beginning; but the end thereof shall not be blessed.

22. Say not thou, I will recompense evil; but wait on the Lord, and he shall save thee.

23. Divers weights are an abomination unto the Lord; and a false balance is not good.

24. Man's goings are of the Lord; how can a man then understand his own way?

25. It is a snare to the man who devoureth that which is holy, and after vows to make enquiry.

26. A wise king scattereth the wicked, and bringeth the wheel over them.

27. The spirit of man is the candle of the Lord, searching all the inward parts of the belly.

28. Mercy and truth preserve the king: and his throne is upholden by mercy.

29. The glory of young men is their strength: and the beauty of old men is the grey head.

30. The blueness of a wound cleanseth away evil: so do stripes the inward parts of the belly.

He who curses . . . A father teaches his son Torah, while a mother instructs him in how to perform Mitzvoth and act righteously. Concerning these two roles, the verse states: "For a commandment is a candle, Torah is a light." (Proverbs 6:23) Therefore, a person who rejects the teachings of his father dwells in darkness, without the light of Torah knowledge. If he rejects his mother, he will lack even a candle and will dwell in pitch darkness.

An inheritance hastily acquired. . . As with the descendants of Ruben and Gad, who hastened to take the land conquered by the Israelites east of the

Jordan River as their tribal (Numbers 32:1-5). In the end, this territory was the first to be conquered by the Assyrians. One with godly integrity will leave to God the place of revenge for harshness suffered at the hand of others.

<u>Two different weights.</u> Aside from its literal meaning, the verse reproves those who behave piously when in the company of others, but sin when done.

<u>A snare.</u> Transgressions.

<u>He must seek . . . holy vows.</u> In order to make amends for having sinned, he must declare holy vows and beseech God for forgiveness. Words expressing religious commitment often come easily. Fulfillment of promises made may bring sorrow and personal loss (Judges 11:29-39). We must not trap ourselves with our words.

<u>A wise king . . .</u> He separates the wicked from each other to prevent them from conferring together, and he punishes them in kind for their sins.

<u>The soul of man . . .</u> When the time comes for a man to be judged by his maker, his soul discloses the thoughts and intentions which were concealed in the inner most recessed of consciousness. The soul discloses everything that a man did in public and in private.

PROVERBS 21

1. The king's heart is in the hand of the Lord, as the rivers of water: he turneth it whithersoever he will.

2. Every way of a man is right in his own eyes: but the Lord pondereth the hearts.

3. To do justice and judgment is more acceptable to the Lord than sacrifice.

4. An high look, and a proud heart, and the plowing of the wicked, is sin.

5. The thoughts of the diligent tend only to plenteousness; but of every one that is hasty only to want.

6. The getting of treasures by a lying tongue is a vanity tossed to and fro of them that seek death.

7. The robbery of the wicked shall destroy them; because they refuse to do judgment.

8. The way of man is froward and strange: but as for the pure, his work is right.

9. It is better to dwell in a corner of the housetop, than with a brawling woman in a wide house.

10. The soul of the wicked desireth evil: his neighbour findeth no favour in his eyes.

The heart of a King . . . Just as water in a glass can be tilted in any direction, when a man rises to the throne, his heat is in the hands of God. If the people are worthy, God inclines the heart of the King to do good. If the people are not worthy, God inclines his heart to establish harsh decrees, each one of which emanates from God.

Verse one, expresses confidence in the sovereignty of God, His ultimate control over all things. Acts of worship play a central role in biblical teaching, but they remain secondary through all parts of scripture to the call for righteousness and justice.

Haughty eyes and a greedy heart. Arrogance ("haughty eyes") and intense craving for physical pleasures ("a greedy heart") constitutes the sinful mind-set of the wicked.

The thoughts . . . Aside from the plain meaning, the verse also teaches the proper method of Torah study: A person who is goal-oriented and diligently reviews the material he has learned will always gain. But someone who sets out to accumulate as much knowledge as possible in the shortest time, will end up with nothing.

A wind-swept mist . . . his death. Such treasures will not last long, and will also bring about their owner's death prematurely.

The stolen possession . . . "The iniquity of the wicked terrifies them . . . " – referring to corrupt judges. They will be victims of their own corruption, for their unwillingness to establish law and order will bring about an increase in crime.

The ways of man divergent and strange. The man who steals not only rejects the notion of justice but has trouble with the accepted norms of society and the natural tendencies of man in general.

<u>Better to dwell . . .</u> The "quarrelsome wife" represents the Jewish people, and the "house of a friend" alludes to the idolatry brought into the Holy Temple (the idolators saw their idols as friends to the Almighty.)

11. When the scorner is punished, the simple is made wise: and when the wise is instructed, he receiveth knowledge.

12. The righteous man wisely considereth the house of the wicked: but God overthroweth the wicked for their wickedness.

13. Whoso stoppeth his ears at the cry of the poor, he also shall cry himself, but shall not be heard.

14. A gift in secret pacifieth anger: and a reward in the bosom strong wrath.

15. It is joy to the just to do judgment: but destruction shall be to the workers of iniquity.

<u>A wise man . . . acquire knowledge.</u> He does not need adversity to motivate him ot improve; a little instruction suffices. Thereafter, he will on his own add to the knowledge he already possesses.

God's wisdom leads to self-discipline through the power of His spirit and the teaching of His word.

<u>The righteous . . .</u> "The righteous" refers to God who formulates plans to destroy the wicked.

<u>A gift in secret suppresses . . . wrath.</u> The verse teaches that acts of charity suppresses God's anger. But that's if a person refrains from giving charity, He will ultimately be forces to give and equivalent sum ot the authorities.

16. he man that wandereth out of the way of understanding shall remain in the congregation of the dead.

17. He that loveth pleasure shall be a poor man: he that loveth wine and oil shall not be rich.

18. The wicked shall be a ransom for the righteous, and the transgressor for the upright.

19. It is better to dwell in the wilderness, than with a contentious and an angry woman.

20. There is treasure to be desired and oil in the dwelling of the wise; but a foolish man spendeth it up.

21. He that followeth after righteousness and mercy findeth life, righteousness, and honour.

22. A wise man scaleth the city of the mighty, and casteth down the strength of the confidence thereof.

23. Whoso keepeth his mouth and his tongue keepeth his soul from troubles.

24. Proud and haughty scorner is his name, who dealeth in proud wrath.

25. The desire of the slothful killeth him; for his hands refuse to labour.

The way of enlightenment. The Torah.

In the company of the dead. Gehinnom. Not merit being resurrected with the revival of the dead.

The wicked man. . . When a righteous person evokes calamity, a wicked person is made to suffer in his stead. The Quintessential example of this principle is Haman, who was hung in pace of Mordechai.

<u>Precious treasure</u> . . . A wise man sets aside provisions for time of need, but a food consumes everything that comes his way.

<u>He who pursues charity</u> . . . This teaches that when a person pursues charity, God provides him with sufficient money to give charitably. God provides him with worthy people with whom to do charity.

<u>A wise man</u> . . . This verse teaches that wisdom is more powerful than physical strength and courage. It also alludes to Moses' ascent to the heavens, where he struggled against the angels and overcame them. (Exodus 43:2) The soul of every righteous man ascends to the heavens during sleep and learns Torah there.

<u>The evil doer</u> . . . <u>crosses all bounds.</u> The evil doer here is someone who rejects the Torah's view of what constitutes wisdom and faith and denies divine providence and the principles of reward and punishment. If such a person does not become haughty, he can be reasoned with. His haughtiness, however, turns him into a scoffer, after which his maliciousness knows no bounds.

26. He coveteth greedily all the day long: but the righteous giveth and spareth not.

27. The sacrifice of the wicked is abomination: how much more, when he bringeth it with a wicked mind?

28. A false witness shall perish: but the man that heareth speaketh constantly.

29. A wicked man hardeneth his face: but as for the upright, he directeth his way.

30. There is no wisdom nor understanding nor counsel against the Lord.

31. The horse is prepared against the day of battle: but safety is of the Lord.

Dr. Gilbert H. Edwards, Sr.

Righteousness and justice demand that all citizens work hard and make positive contributions to society.

The wicked, who expresses no remorse for his sins, hoping that his sacrifices alone will suffice.

With evil intention. For example, "Balak and Balaam", who offered a sacrifice to God for the express purpose of bringing a course upon the Jewish people.

The worth of one's gift is measured by the spirit and intent of the giver. Wicked, godless persons think they can maintain a proper relationship with God through observing worship rituals and giving enough money to God's work. They are wrong. God measures by intention and attitude rather than by amount. We must serve God, not selfish ambition.

Who listens, to the Torah commandment? "Do not testify as a false witness against your neighbor." (Exodus 20:15)

Is prudent. He behaves disrespectfully towards his fellow men, and he commits sins against God.

Understanding His way. He remains in control even when he feels anger.

There is no wisdom . . . Even the wisest men are totally insignificant before God. Verse 30 teaches that even someone who has attained these three qualities is incapable of revoking a heavenly decree.

The horse is ready . . . A person may ready the means by which to escape from the enemy, but unless God decrees that he be saved it will be of no avail to him; for salvation rests solely in the hands of God.

112

PROVERBS 22

1. A good name is rather to be chosen than great riches, and loving favour rather than silver and gold.

2. The rich and poor meet together: the Lord is the maker of them all.

3. A prudent man foreseeth the evil, and hideth himself: but the simple pass on, and are punished.

4. By humility and the fear of the Lord are riches, and honour, and life.

5. Thorns and snares are in the way of the froward: he that doth keep his soul shall be far from them.

6. Train up a child in the way he should go: and when he is old, he will not depart from it.

7. The rich ruleth over the poor, and the borrower is servant to the lender.

Better a good name . . . God makes them all. One ought not admire the rich and sneer at the poor, since human beings – even the most intelligent and skilled – are not in control of wealth. Rich and poor alike only "meet" the fate which God has decreed for them. In contrast, "a good name" and "a pleasing demeanor" are earned entirely through ones' own efforts, and therefore are more precious than even "a great fortune."

Wealth and poverty may appear to show that creation is unfair and unjust. Such differences are extinguished when people stand before their Creator. He made every person and treats all with justice.

On the heels of humility . . . The fear of God is only the heel of humility. Most see the fear of God as the more exalted; only by perfecting one's humility can the fear of God be attained.

Educate the youngster . . . No matter how hard one may try, one cannot change one's temperament. Man's "free will" only enables him to choose whether he uses the natural tendencies with which he was endowed to pursue good or to pursue evil.

This verse six warns against training youngsters to perform Mitzvoth through methods which run contrary to his nature. True, when he is young, he can be forced to obey, but as soon as he matures enough to assert his independence, he will reject everything his parents taught him. The only way to impart to one's child a fondness for Mitzvoth, which will not wave "even when he grows old" is to "educate the youngster according to His way!"

Indebtedness is a kind of slavery. Over extension of credit without an appropriate repayment agreement can mean loss of one's possessions, one's reputation, and if a constant theme of life, loss of one's integrity. To become rich and exercise oppressive rule over the helpless poor is not the goal of life.

8. He that soweth iniquity shall reap vanity: and the rod of his anger shall fail.

9. He that hath a bountiful eye shall be blessed; for he giveth of his bread to the poor.

10. Cast out the scorner, and contention shall go out; yea, strife and reproach shall cease.

11. He that loveth pureness of heart, for the grace of his lips the king shall be his friend.

12. The eyes of the Lord preserve knowledge, and he over throweth the words of the transgressor.

13. The slothful man saith, There is a lion without, I shall be slain in the streets.

14. The mouth of strange women is a deep pit: he that is abhorred of the Lord shall fall therein.

<u>Rod of His anger.</u> A metaphor reference to his oppressive control over others, or to his abusive anger.

<u>A generous man . . .</u> God blesses a generous person with prosperity in order to give him the ability to perform even greater acts of generosity.

The caring person who enjoy helping others receive blessings abundantly. Jesus taught that giving brings the reward of inward blessings. Stewardship involves a caring attitude that leads to caring actions for people in need.

<u>The scoffer.</u> An allusion to the evil inclination – International war grows out of persona strife. Such strife roots in insecure people who mock the achievements of others and in jealousy fight for undeserved attention. Society begins the road to peace when it helps these people change their ways.

<u>God loves . . .</u> One who knows truth and knows how to communicate truth tactfully will have many supporters.

<u>He distorts the words . . .</u> He foils the evil schemes which "the treacherous" plot against "men of knowledge."

<u>The lazy man says . . .</u> He invents preposterous excuses to avoid working for a living. Those who do not wish to work will always find an excuse for not doing so.

<u>The mouth of the woman stranger.</u> Representing idolatry or heretical beliefs.

15. Foolishness is bound in the heart of a child; but the rod of correction shall drive it far from him.

16. He that oppresseth the poor to increase his riches, and he that giveth to the rich, shall surely come to want.

17. Bow down thine ear, and hear the words of the wise, and apply thine heart unto my knowledge.

18. For it is a pleasant thing if thou keep them within thee; they shall withal be fitted in thy lips.

19. That thy trust may be in the Lord, I have made known to thee this day, even to thee.

20. Have not I written to thee excellent things in counsels and knowledge,

21. That I might make thee know the certainty of the words of truth; that thou mightest answer the words of truth to them that send unto thee?

22. Rob not the poor, because he is poor: neither oppress the afflicted in the gate:

23. For the Lord will plead their cause, and spoil the soul of those that spoiled them.

24. Make no friendship with an angry man; and with a furious man thou shalt not go:

25. Lest thou learn his ways, and get a snare to thy soul.

26. Be not thou one of them that strike hands, or of them that are sureties for debts.

27. If thou hast nothing to pay, why should he take away thy bed from under thee?

28. Remove not the ancient landmark, which thy fathers have set.

29. Seest thou a man diligent in his business? he shall stand before kings; he shall not stand before mean men.

Concentrate on knowing me. As the scripture states: Let not the wise man glory in his wisdom, or the strong man glory in his strength; or the rich man glory in his riches. Only in this should one glory: in his devotion to me." (Jeremiah 9:22)

The learner's self-discipline is more important than external imposed discipline. The presence of good teaching does not guarantee learning, for learning is an active process in which learners seek truth and apply themselves to the task. Indifference, self-sufficiency, or dullness of mind and heart can close our ears to words of wisdom. We do not acquire knowledge by sitting passively and waiting for it. We must search for it as though it were a hidden treasure.

Safeguard them in your words, so as not to forget the words of Torah you have learned.

Place your trust in God . . . Study Torah diligently, without worrying about earning a living. Trust in God and have faith that he will provide all your needs. The verse teaches that one of the essential aims of Torah study is to develop faith in God.

A threefold lore. The Pentateuch, prophets and sacred writings, or a reference to the Book of Proverbs itself, which is divided into three parts.

Who led you astray? "Who sent you off?" or "Who asked you legal queries?" or, "Who escorted you-in this world?" – a reference to the written or oral Torah.

<u>Do not rob the poor man</u> . . . But does a poor man own anything worth robbing? Rather, the verse teaches that if you sustain him on a regular basis and then decide to stop, it is considered as if you "stole" from him.

Beginning in infancy, human beings learn by imitating the behavior of others. The examples others get are not always positive. The biblical writer had this in mind when he warned against association with persons who are habitually angry. Negative emotions are contagious. Unfortunately, children whose parents are temperamental have no choice in the matter. Brought up under the daily influence of angry parents, they learn to be hot tempered people themselves. By self-discipline and associating with the right people, we can unlearn bad habits acquired as children. We cannot blame our problems on our parents. We must take responsibility for ourselves and take full responsibility for ourselves and set good examples for our families, friends and associates.

<u>Do not set back.</u> . . . Continue in the ways of your forefathers even if they are at odds with the accepted norms of your day.

<u>Do you see a man</u> . . . A superb artisan working exclusively for a King would not even contemplate quitting his position in order to do unskilled work for coarse men who cannot recognize his talents.

PROVERBS 23

1. When thou sittest to eat with a ruler, consider diligently what is before thee:

2. And put a knife to thy throat, if thou be a man given to appetite.

3. Be not desirous of his dainties: for they are deceitful meat.

4. Labour not to be rich: cease from thine own wisdom.

5. Wilt thou set thine eyes upon that which is not? for riches certainly make themselves wings; they fly away as an eagle toward heaven.

6. Eat thou not the bread of him that hath an evil eye, neither desire thou his dainty meats:

7. For as he thinketh in his heart, so is he: Eat and drink, saith he to thee; but his heart is not with thee.

8. The morsel which thou hast eaten shalt thou vomit up, and lose thy sweet words.

9. Speak not in the ears of a fool: for he will despise the wisdom of thy words.

10. Remove not the old landmark; and enter not into the fields of the fatherless:

Dr. Gilbert H. Edwards, Sr.

When you sit down . . . If you determine that your host is a miser, it is better to stick a knife in your throat than to eat his food. Alternatively, "ruler" alludes to the evil inclination, which entices people to sin by offering them sensual "delicacies" to stop yourself from dining on "the ruler's" delicacies, stick a knife in your throat.

Desist of your own understanding. The father in essence says to his son, "You should have had enough sense on your own to deduce the futility of toiling for riches"; or, "stop misusing your power of understanding to amass wealth!" Alternatively, "Do not toil to become rich, for you will desist from your understanding" – the outcome of toiling for wealth is that one loses one's Torah knowledge.

Muses. His offer to partake of his food is as insubstantial as the absent-minded musing which cross a man's mind. Wealth for its own sake is deceptive in its promise of satisfaction. It leads to the loss of personal integrity and values serving the rich and powerful, to fleeting success with riches which do not provide the emotional and spiritual riches we seek, or to deception and dishonesty.

Do not set back . . . Here, the verse emphasizes the importance of observing the commandments which prescribe the amount of produce to be set aside for the poor. (Leviticus 23:22)

11. For their redeemer is mighty; he shall plead their cause with thee.

12. Apply thine heart unto instruction, and thine ears to the words of knowledge.

13. Withhold not correction from the child: for if thou beatest him with the rod, he shall not die.

14. Thou shalt beat him with the rod, and shalt deliver his soul from hell.

15. My son, if thine heart be wise, my heart shall rejoice, even mine.

16. Yea, my reins shall rejoice, when thy lips speak right things.

17. Let not thine heart envy sinners: but be thou in the fear of the Lord all the day long.

18. For surely there is an end; and thine expectation shall not be cut off.

Because their redeemer . . . As scripture warns: "Do not mistreat a widow or an orphan. If you mistreat them and they cry out to Me, I will hear their cry. I will-then-display My anger and kill you by the sword, so that your wives will be widows and your children orphans." (Exodus 22:21-23).

If you strike him . . . As if to say, "Don't worry, your blows won't kill him" or the verse teaches that by educating one's children in Torah, one prevents their eternal soul from expiring at the times of their corporal death.

My heart, too, will rejoice. Parents and children have common spiritual roots, and so a parent is capable of perceiving his child's wisdom even if the child never gives expression to it. Therefore, as long as his child's "heart is wise", the parent will inexplicably be filled with joy. A necessary responsibility of parents is disciplining children. This training prepares them for life, bringing satisfaction to the parents.

But only those who . . . or, "but occupy yourself with the fear of God all day long."

You will thus . . . The very fact that there is reason to envy the wicked proves this point – if God deemed it fit to reward the wicked in this world, then surely He will also reward the righteous.

19. Hear thou, my son, and be wise, and guide thine heart in the way.

20. Be not among winebibbers; among riotous eaters of flesh:

21. For the drunkard and the glutton shall come to poverty: and drowsiness shall clothe a man with rags.

22. Hearken unto thy father that begat thee, and despise not thy mother when she is old.

23. Buy the truth, and sell it not; also wisdom, and instruction, and understanding.

24. The father of the righteous shall greatly rejoice: and he that begetteth a wise child shall have joy of him.

25. Thy father and thy mother shall be glad, and she that bare thee shall rejoice.

<u>Guzzle wine and glut themselves on meat</u>. Referring to individuals who spend their days pursuing earthly pleasures.

<u>Purchase truth . . .</u> One should make an effort to purchase holy works and avoid relinquishing ownership by reselling them, or a person who is unable to find someone to teach him Torah for free should "purchase truth by hiring a teacher." When this person becomes a scholar, he may reason that since he paid for his Torah knowledge, he is fully justified in charging others for lessons. To this, the verse says, "do not sell it."

<u>A wise child</u>, a teacher of Torah.

<u>She who bore you. . . .</u> The one who helped you brar and "give birth to" the wisdom inside your heart.

26. My son, give me thine heart, and let thine eyes observe my ways.

27. For a whore is a deep ditch; and a strange woman is a narrow pit.

28. She also lieth in wait as for a prey, and increaseth the transgressors among men.

29. Who hath woe? who hath sorrow? who hath contentions? who hath babbling? who hath wounds without cause? who hath redness of eyes?

30. They that tarry long at the wine; they that go to seek mixed wine.

31. Look not thou upon the wine when it is red, when it giveth his colour in the cup, when it moveth itself aright.

32. At the last it biteth like a serpent, and stingeth like an adder.

33. Thine eyes shall behold strange women, and thine heart shall utter perverse things.

34. Yea, thou shalt be as he that lieth down in the midst of the sea, or as he that lieth upon the top of a mast.

35. They have stricken me, shalt thou say, and I was not sick; they have beaten me, and I felt it not: when shall I awake? I will seek it yet again.

<u>The harlot . . .</u> A person who has embraced heretical beliefs finds it as difficult to disentangle himself from them, as a devoted patron from a harlot.

<u>To whom woe . . .</u> A person who has taken to drinking harms the members of his household, his relatives, and his acquaintances. The members of his household experience "woe" when he stops earning a livelihood, and "grief" when they go hungry; his relatives experience "strife" when they quarrel with him, and in his absence incessantly "chatter" about his misbehavior; his acquaintances suffer physical "wounds" when they encounter him in the midst of one of his drunken rampages, and their eyes become "bleary" from laughter when ridiculing him in public.

PROVERBS 24

1. Be not thou envious against evil men, neither desire to be with them.

2. For their heart studieth destruction, and their lips talk of mischief.

3. Through wisdom is an house builded; and by understanding it is established:

4. And by knowledge shall the chambers be filled with all precious and pleasant riches.

5. A wise man is strong; yea, a man of knowledge increaseth strength.

6. For by wise counsel thou shalt make thy war: and in multitude of counsellors there is safety.

7. Wisdom is too high for a fool: he openeth not his mouth in the gate.

8. He that deviseth to do evil shall be called a mischievous person.

9. The thought of foolishness is sin: and the scorner is an abomination to men.

10. If thou faint in the day of adversity, thy strength is small.

<u>A wise man is strong</u> . . . A wise man's fear of God is steadfast and remains on a constant level, whereas a man of knowledge is capable of increasing his fear of God by means of his Torah knowledge.

<u>You wage war</u>, against evil inclination.

<u>To the fool</u> . . . The fool thinks Torah knowledge is beyond his reach. He says to himself, "How can I study Torah? When will I ever master it?" The wise man on the other hand studies a little every day until in time, he has mastered the entire Torah.

<u>They call him a schemer.</u> He causes harm to himself by earning a bad reputation.

<u>A foolish scheme is a crime.</u> To the one who conceived it, for it brings about his demise.

<u>If you are lax</u> . . . If you neglect assisting a friend who is experiencing hardship, you will be punished in kind.

When adversity befalls you, you will lack the necessary strength to extricate yourself from danger. This is as in, "If you persist on keeping silent at a time like this, relief and deliverance will come to the Jews from another place when you and your father's house will perish." (Esther 4:14)

11. If thou forbear to deliver them that are drawn unto death, and those that are ready to be slain;

12. If thou sayest, Behold, we knew it not; doth not he that pondereth the heart consider it? and he that keepeth thy soul, doth not he know it? and shall not he render to every man according to his works?

13. My son, eat thou honey, because it is good; and the honeycomb, which is sweet to thy taste:

14. So shall the knowledge of wisdom be unto thy soul: when thou hast found it, then there shall be a reward, and thy expectation shall not be cut off.

15. Lay not wait, O wicked man, against the dwelling of the righteous; spoil not his resting place:

16. For a just man falleth seven times, and riseth up again: but the wicked shall fall into mischief.

17. Rejoice not when thine enemy falleth, and let not thine heart be glad when he stumbleth:

Honey. A metaphor for knowledge, understanding, intelligence and wisdom.

There is a future. That is, you will live to a ripe old age, or merit man's descendants.

For even times . . . As in, "The righteous man experiences many hardships, but God saves him from them all." (Psalms 34:20)

God's wrath is not cause for us to rejoice, that sin would bring His wrath upon us.

18. Lest the Lord see it, and it displease him, and he turn away his wrath from him.

19. Fret not thyself because of evil men, neither be thou envious at the wicked:

20. For there shall be no reward to the evil man; the candle of the wicked shall be put out.

21. My son, fear thou the Lord and the king: and meddle not with them that are given to change:

22. For their calamity shall rise suddenly; and who knoweth the ruin of them both?

23. These things also belong to the wise. It is not good to have respect of persons in judgment.

24. He that saith unto the wicked, Thou are righteous; him shall the people curse, nations shall abhor him:

25. But to them that rebuke him shall be delight, and a good blessing shall come upon them.

26. Every man shall kiss his lips that giveth a right answer.

Fear God . . . and also the King. One should fear God and the King although the fear of God takes priority. Therefore, if the King attempts to turn people away from the fear of God, one should not obey him.

What does "and also the King" mean? It teaches that anyone who fears God earns the statue of a King. From whom do we learn this? From Abraham, about whom the verse says, "For now I know that you fear God." (Genesis 22:12) He was made King when he defeated the four Kings in Shave Valley, which was renamed "King's Valley."

Their. Referring to God and the King both of whom punish those who transgress their decrees, or to those who fail to fear God and the King. The are chastened suddenly and punished without any foreknowledge.

These, too, are ... As is known, it was the men of the great assembly who compiled the words of the prophets into what we know today as the sacred writings.

People will curse him . . . Acquittal emboldens man to commit even more serious crimes, and so his victims will curse the judge who acquitted him.

<u>Who rebuke him pleasantly.</u> Bluntly confronting a wicked man with his evil deeds is likely to make himself defensive so that he might even deny his guilt.

Rather for rebuke to be accepted, it must be stated in a gentle pleasant manner. Begin by assuring the sinner that he is essentially righteous, but he possesses a few minor character flaws, which he should try to rectify, or "Those who rebuke will themselves be pleased," for doing the right thing pleases the soul.

<u>He will purse his lips . . .</u> When rebuke is given as prescribed above, the sinner will hold his silence and refrain from replying in a defiant manner.

Further, he will take the rebuke to heart and identify even more negative traits which he will try to rectify. Truth and honesty have their own satisfying reward.

27. Prepare thy work without, and make it fit for thyself in the field; and afterwards build thine house.

28. Be not a witness against thy neighbour without cause; and deceive not with thy lips.

29. Say not, I will do so to him as he hath done to me: I will render to the man according to his work.

30. I went by the field of the slothful, and by the vineyard of the man void of understanding;

31. And, lo, it was all grown over with thorns, and nettles had covered the face thereof, and the stone wall thereof was broken down.

32. Then I saw, and considered it well: I looked upon it, and received instruction.

33. Yet a little sleep, a little slumber, a little folding of the hands to sleep:

34. So shall thy poverty come as one that travelleth; and thy want as an armed man.

Then build your house, then marry a woman. First build a house, then plant a vineyard, and afterwards take a wife.

Do not be a witness . . . A single witness should not give testimony. If he does, it is considered as if he had "deceived with his lips," i.e., spoken slander.

Even if a neighbor has done us wrong, vengeance is to be left with God (Matthew 5:38-48).

A little sleep . . . The wise person learns from the experience of others.

Laziness and refusal to work not only robs a person of personal accomplishments and meaning, but they also destroy through negligence what previous generations have accomplished. To make "rest" a top priority creates poverty.

PROVERBS 25

1. These are also proverbs of Solomon, which the men of Hezekiah king of Judah copied out.

2. It is the glory of God to conceal a thing: but the honour of kings is to search out a matter.

3. The heaven for height, and the earth for depth, and the heart of kings is unsearchable.

4. Take away the dross from the silver, and there shall come forth a vessel for the finer.

5. Take away the wicked from before the king, and his throne shall be established in righteousness.

6. Put not forth thyself in the presence of the king, and stand not in the place of great men:

7. For better it is that it be said unto thee, Come up hither; than that thou shouldest be put lower in the presence of the prince whom thine eyes have seen.

8. Go not forth hastily to strive, lest thou know not what to do in the end thereof, when thy neighbour hath put thee to shame.

9. Debate thy cause with thy neighbour himself; and discover not a secret to another:

10. Lest he that heareth it put thee to shame, and thine infamy turn not away.

<u>King Hezekiah</u>. The righteous King who restored the honor of the Torah following the death of Ahaz (11 Kings 18).

<u>The honor of God . . .</u> When honoring God, the less one says the better since it is impossible to honor God sufficiently. Conversely when honoring a King, one should speak effusively since it is impossible to honor him sufficiently.

God's revelation gives what His people need to know, not all that could be known about God. The unique nature of God is that He is greater than the human mind and imagination. Even Kings with all their power and human resources cannot search out the mysterious side of God's nature. Work for good and justice. The results will allow others more possibilities for doing work of justice. Wicked advisors can destroy a ruler.

<u>Do not glorify yourself . . .</u> Aside from its literal meaning, the verse warns Christians against interjecting their own opinions in the presence of a Torah Master.

<u>In the place of great men</u>. A Christian should not choose a teacher who is so erudite that he cannot even comprehend his lessons. Instead, he should study under a teacher of lesser renown, accumulate knowledge, and then attempt once again to understand his first teacher's words.

<u>As your own eyes have seen</u>. As you yourself must know from experience.

<u>Fight your battle . . .</u> If you must quarrel, do so but do not use underhanded tactics like embarrassing your opponent by revealing secrets about him – such as his ancestors' shortcomings.

11. A word fitly spoken is like apples of gold in pictures of silver.

12. As an earring of gold, and an ornament of fine gold, so is a wise reprover upon an obedient ear.

13. As the cold of snow in the time of harvest, so is a faithful messenger to them that send him: for he refresheth the soul of his masters.

14. Whoso boasteth himself of a false gift is like clouds and wind without rain.

15. By long forbearing is a prince persuaded, and a soft tongue breaketh the bone.

16. Hast thou found honey? eat so much as is sufficient for thee, lest thou be filled therewith, and vomit it.

17. Withdraw thy foot from thy neighbour's house; lest he be weary of thee, and so hate thee.

18. A man that beareth false witness against his neighbour is a maul, and a sword, and a sharp arrow.

19. Confidence in an unfaithful man in time of trouble is like a broken tooth, and a foot out of joint.

<u>A harvest day</u>. The harvest season usually coincides with the peak of summer heat. Though cool weather is expected pleasure.

<u>A messenger who is faithful</u>. Alluding to Caleb, son of Yefuneh, who was "faithful" to Moses and Joshua when they sent him to explore the promised land, and who restored "is Master's spirit" by causing the Divine providence to return to the Land of Israel.

<u>Like clouds . . .</u> Someone who makes false pledges to charity in order to gain honor has the same effect as clouds and wind on a rainless day during a year of drought – he initially raises people's hopes, but then plunges them even deeper in despair.

A message appropriately delivered can lift our spirits. One who boasts actually declares his emptiness of spirit. Unfaithful words wear us out; good news refreshes us.

A ruler is won over . . . Bearing the anger of a ruler in silence wins his favor and dispels his wrath. When a ruler shows forbearance, his enemies seize the opportunity and immediately take advantage of him, or when God shows forbearance, the wicked are presented with the opportunity to appease Hi8m through repentance and prayer.

A soft tongue breaks bones. When a ruler does not show forbearance and remains unyielding as a "bone" softly spoken, please will eventually break through his horrid demeanor and touch his heart.

Restrict your visits. "Make your feet scarce in your friend's house."

Self-discipline leads to moderation in all of life. To falsely convict a person of a crime, is to fight a war against our neighbor.

Like a broken tooth . . . That in which the wicked man trusts will fail on the day of adversity.

20. As he that taketh away a garment in cold weather, and as vinegar upon nitre, so is he that singeth songs to an heavy heart.

21. If thine enemy be hungry, give him bread to eat; and if he be thirsty, give him water to drink:

22. For thou shalt heap coals of fire upon his head, and the Lord shall reward thee.

23. The north wind driveth away rain: so doth an angry countenance a backbiting tongue.

24. It is better to dwell in the corner of the housetop, than with a brawling woman and in a wide house.

25. As cold waters to a thirsty soul, so is good news from a far country.

26. A righteous man falling down before the wicked is as a troubled fountain, and a corrupt spring.

27. It is not good to eat much honey: so for men to search their own glory is not glory.

28. He that hath no rule over his own spirit is like a city that is broken down, and without walls.

A threadbare garment, or "removing one's garment", or "an elegant garment", which offers no protection against the elements.

On delicate earthware, or, "mixed with soft earth used for cleaning garments."

Embittered soul, or "a man of evil heart." The verse warns against teaching Torah to a wicked Christian who has no intention of fulfilling its Laws.

If your enemy . . . That is, do not bear a grudge against him, or the verse teaches how to overcome one's evil inclination: If it should grow hungry and thirsty for physical pleasures, take it to the study hall and feed it "the bread" and "the water" of Torah.

Secretive talk . . . Slanderous talk kindles God's wrath against the one who speaks it, or it causes others to look angrily upon the subject of the slanderer.

Like cold water . . . As in the verse, "then they related all the words that Joseph had spoken to them . . . The spirit of their father Jacob was then revived." (Genesis 45:27)

Like a spring trodden over . . . When a righteous person refrains from rebuking a wicked one due to fear, it is as despicable as muddy water, or the verse metaphorically describes the consequences of allowing one's evil inclination to gain the upper hand.

Probing . . . is an honor. The wisdom of the righteous is their honor. The more people probe the wisdom of their teachings, the better.

Proverbs 26

1. As snow in summer, and as rain in harvest, so honour is not seemly for a fool.

2. As the bird by wandering, as the swallow by flying, so the curse causeless shall not come.

3. A whip for the horse, a bridle for the ass, and a rod for the fool's back.

4. Answer not a fool according to his folly, lest thou also be like unto him.

5. Answer a fool according to his folly, lest he be wise in his own conceit.

6. He that sendeth a message by the hand of a fool cutteth off the feet, and drinketh damage.

7. The legs of the lame are not equal: so is a parable in the mouth of fools.

8. As he that bindeth a stone in a sling, so is he that giveth honour to a fool.

9. As a thorn goeth up into the hand of a drunkard, so is a parable in the mouths of fools.

10. The great God that formed all things both rewardeth the fool, and rewardeth transgressors.

Honor unfitting for a fool. For if he is shown, people will think there is not advantage to gaining wisdom.

Like a bird that wanders . . . Just as birds and swallows when driven from their nests inevitable return, so undeserved curses always backfires again the imprecator.

Language does not give us unlimited power. To place another person under an undeserved curse has no effect on the other person. It does reveal the foolishness of the speaker.

A rod. This is the hardship instore for evil doers. However, there is a great difference between these two beasts and the fool: it is unnecessary to actually strike the horse on the ass – the horses increases speed at the mere sight of the whip and moved by the searing pain of actual blows.

Do not respond to a fool's folly in kind. This verse discusses how to behave in the fact of provocation, such as when one is being cursed by a fool.

Respond . . . in kind. This verse describes how to react to a person who is attempting to lead one astray; or, to a person who has misconstrued a Torah principle.

He who sends a message . . . The foolish messenger will distort the message and unwittingly cause a terrible misunderstanding to develop between the sender and the receiver. The sender will need to dispatch a series of messengers to resolve the misunderstanding, thereby "tiring out" their legs in the process.

The careful listener recognizes a foolish speaker. It is a losing battle to attempt to engage with such people on their level. The mature person in God attempts to raise the level of conversation and to guide the fool away from foolish conceit.

<u>Like thighs appear high up . . .</u> Just as cripples hobbling on the ground regard people's thighs out of reach, so fools regard the attainment of wisdom beyond people's grasp.

<u>Like a stone . . .</u> Just as stone does not stay in the sling for long before it is hurled, so the honor shown to a fool does not endure for long before it is driven away by a foolish at.

<u>A proverb in the mouth of fools</u>. The "proverbs" of foolish men are as damaging to themselves as to others; or the verse illustrates the difficulty fools experience in understanding the Book of Proverbs. Just as a thorn embedded in the hand of a drunkard can be visible to all yet impossible to extract because of the drunkard's erratic movements; so the fool may be well-versed in proverbs yet find it impossible to extract the moral lessons encased therein.

<u>The belligerent man . . .</u> Although a belligerent man harms all those who come within his reach, he befriends fools and transgressors by hiring them to work for him, thereby gaining their allegiance.

11. As a dog returneth to his vomit, so a fool returneth to his folly.

12. Seest thou a man wise in his own conceit? there is more hope of a fool than of him.

13. The slothful man saith, There is a lion in the way; a lion is in the streets.

14. As the door turneth upon his hinges, so doth the slothful upon his bed.

15. The slothful hideth his hand in his bosom; it grieveth him to bring it again to his mouth.

16. The sluggard is wiser in his own conceit than seven men that can render a reason.

17. He that passeth by, and meddleth with strife belonging not to him, is like one that taketh a dog by the ears.

18. As a mad man who casteth firebrands, arrows, and death,

19. So is the man that deceiveth his neighbour, and saith, Am not I in sport?

20. Where no wood is, there the fire goeth out: so where there is no talebearer, the strife ceaseth.

Genuine wisdom recognizes its own limitations and is ready to learn more. Self-center4d pride robs us of the change to improve.

<u>The lazy man . . .</u> He makes all kinds of preposterous excuses in order to avoid having to go out to work. (Ezra 15:19; 22:13)

<u>A lazy man turns in his bed.</u> Just as the door swings on its hinges, yet remain firmly attached to the wall, so a lazy man turns to and fro in his bed but does not rise; or the door swings on its hingers, but the lazy man is on his bed. When most people are already bustling about and causing doors to swing on their hinges, the lazy man has yet to rise.

<u>One who seizes a dog by its ears.</u> He causes injury to himself.

<u>Sparks of fire.</u> Referring to firearms.

<u>Death.</u> That is, instrument of death.

<u>So is the man . . .</u> His intentions are as malicious as those of the murderer described in verse 18. This is a metaphor for the evil inclination: it befriends a person and entices him to sin, then after the individual has committed the congression, it hurls harsh punishment at him.

Making jokes at another's expense shows foolishness. Playing on other's emotions and intentions is dishonest and malicious. We need to find better ways to gain attention. How do we treat gossip? We are not to give it credence by ever responding to it. Such an approach will soon see the end of gossip and cause us to avoid fights with other people.

21. As coals are to burning coals, and wood to fire; so is a contentious man to kindle strife.

22. The words of a talebearer are as wounds, and they go down into the innermost parts of the belly.

23. Burning lips and a wicked heart are like a potsherd covered with silver dross.

24. He that hateth dissembleth with his lips, and layeth up deceit within him;

25. When he speaketh fair, believe him not: for there are seven abominations in his heart.

26. Whose hatred is covered by deceit, his wickedness shall be shewed before the whole congregation.

27. Whoso diggeth a pit shall fall therein: and he that rolleth a stone, it will return upon him.

28. A lying tongue hateth those that are afflicted by it; and a flattering mouth worketh ruin.

Deceptive lips. "Pursuing lips" or "burning lips'"

Like plating . . . and an evil heart. Just as the sheen of impure silver can make an earthen ware vessel seem valuable, so a wicked man's deceptive lips can make him seem a trusted friend although he is in fact a sworn enemy. The verse refers to those who study and pray with feigned enthusiasm but remain inwardly unmoved.

A loathsome deed. A deed which is loathsome to God – a transgression.

He who digs a pit . . . A certain man was once clearing his field and casting the stones onto public property. A pious man saw and asked, "Why do you throw that which does not belong to you into that which does not belong to you?" The man scoffed at the pious man's words. In time, the man's fortune took a turn for the worse, and he had no choice but to sell his field. While walking on the public thoroughfare adjacent to the field he once owned, he injured himself on the very stones he had thrown out years earlier. He suddenly remembered the pious man's words – now the field was no longer his, and public property was his home. This is the meaning of "He who digs a pit will fall into it." He who rolls a stone will have it returned to him. (Ecclesiastes 6:11)

A lying tongue . . . For he assumes his victims have become aware of his crime and now consider him their enemy.

Flattery brings respite. For is his victims flatter him and show no trace of bitterness, he assumes they still have not learned of his lies, and so his animosity quickly dissipates.

Language can deceive for a while. We need to refuse to trust charmers whose hearts oppose their lips. Charming lies can win the speaker and other people. Eventually the charmer is found out. We need to resist all temptations to speak anything but the truth.

PROVERBS 27

1. Boast not thyself of to morrow; for thou knowest not what a day may bring forth.

2. Let another man praise thee, and not thine own mouth; a stranger, and not thine own lips.

3. A stone is heavy, and the sand weighty; but a fool's wrath is heavier than them both.

4. Wrath is cruel, and anger is outrageous; but who is able to stand before envy?

5. Open rebuke is better than secret love.

6. Faithful are the wounds of a friend; but the kisses of an enemy are deceitful.

7. The full soul loatheth an honeycomb; but to the hungry soul every bitter thing is sweet.

8. As a bird that wandereth from her nest, so is a man that wandereth from his place.

9. Ointment and perfume rejoice the heart: so doth the sweetness of a man's friend by hearty counsel.

10. Thine own friend, and thy father's friend, forsake not; neither go into thy brother's house in the day of thy calamity: for better is a neighbour that is near than a brother far off.

Tomorrow. Tomorrow's accomplishments.

Let a stranger . . . When a person lowers himself, the Holy One raises him up.

Individual hope does not come in length of days or accomplishment of all plans. God controls each individual's destiny. We will never fulfill all of our plans. Our only source of pride and security is in God.

The heaviness of sand. Although sand is light, its dense volume makes it difficult to carry. It is similarly difficult to bear the long-lasting anger of a fool.

The anger of a fool. The heavenly anger which a fool evokes through his deeds; or a fool's violent outbursts.

The cruelty of rage . . . An enraged man acts cruelly, and one overcome by wrath can be as destructive as a rushing flood. Yet a jealous man is worse, for even willing to forgo personal gain and endure hardship if it will prevent others from being better off than he.

Better open rebuke than love concealed. "For whomever God loves, He rebukes." This principle can be understood through the following analogy: A father who sees his son behaving improperly immediately rebukes him, and if necessary, spanks him in order to rectify his ways. Open rebuke is good from hidden love or, rebuke given in public is more effective than given in private by a loved one.

Are forthright. They are inflicted for a constructive purpose – to rectify that person's faults.

A person who is satisfied . . . For those who are satisfied with their lot in life, luxuries (honey) have no appeal. Conversely, those who are satisfied with what they have are so blinded by avarice that they find even the bitter pursuit after wealth "sweet."

Like a bird . . . Just as it is difficult for a bird to leave its nest, it is difficult for a man to have to travel away from home.

Is better than one's own counsel, or "is from the depths of his being."

Your friend . . . your father's friend. Also alluding to God. If one abandons Him, he is severely punished.

A close neighbor is better . . . A neighbor who is close to you will be more willing to help than a brother who is distant and does not sympathize with your problems. Therefore, do not abandon your friends. Everyone needs friends who are supportive and honest.

11. My son, be wise, and make my heart glad, that I may answer him that reproacheth me.

12. A prudent man foreseeth the evil, and hideth himself; but the simple pass on, and are punished.

13. Take his garment that is surety for a stranger, and take a pledge of him for a strange woman.

14. He that blesseth his friend with a loud voice, rising early in the morning, it shall be counted a curse to him.

15. A continual dropping in a very rainy day and a contentious woman are alike.

16. Whosoever hideth her hideth the wind, and the ointment of his right hand, which bewrayeth itself.

17. Iron sharpeneth iron; so a man sharpeneth the countenance of his friend.

18. Whoso keepeth the fig tree shall eat the fruit thereof: so he that waiteth on his master shall be honoured.

19. As in water face answereth to face, so the heart of man to man.

20. Hell and destruction are never full; so the eyes of man are never satisfied.

<u>That I may have a reply . . .</u> Otherwise, I will have to keep silent, for fear that they will publicize your inadequacies.

<u>Virtually curses him.</u> By publicly praising a person's generosity one can inadvertently cause him harm; people will assume he is very wealthy and exceedingly generous, and so incessantly pester him for money. And when word of his prosperity reaches the ear of the government, he will have to pay higher taxes.

<u>An annoying leak . . .</u> In stormy weather people are forced to stay indoors. At such times, a leak in the roof can be extremely annoying. Similarly, when a man comes home expecting to get some rest, nothing can be more annoying than a quarrelsome wife pestering him with her incessant ragging.

<u>Conceal the wind.</u> Just as it is impossible to conceal the wind, so a man cannot hope to conceal a quarrelsome wife from the public. Just as the wind howls louder when the window is closed, she grows louder when her husband attempts to conceal her.

<u>The oil . . .</u> Some oil inevitably remains on the hands of the person who has handled it. Thus, just as it is almost impossible to hide oi and claim that one has run out, a man cannot hope to conceal a quarrelsome wife.

<u>Sharpens his friend's countenance.</u> Torah scholars who study together sharpen each other's study skills. Genuine friends in honest discussion whet the skill and wisdom of each other. We can never be so wise that we do not need to learn in dialogue with others of opposing viewpoints.

<u>One man's heart reflected in others.</u> This teaches that people reflect each other's feelings. A person responds affectionately to those whom he thinks are fond of him. Similarly, if a person associates with someone who is feeling happy or sad, he will also begin to feel that way. The spiritual lesson to be gleaned from this verse is that to the same degree a person adheres to God; God will adhere to him.

<u>Just as the nether world . . .</u> Just as a wicked man's eyes never tire from leering at that which he desires, so the nether world and Gehinnom never refuses entry to the souls of the wicked.

No life is without its catastrophes. The last one of which is death, the end of life itself. Human greed is as easily satisfied as the graveyard. A wise person learns the limits of material needs and lives within those rather than constantly responding to the drive of personal wants, which are never satisfied.

21. As the fining pot for silver, and the furnace for gold; so is a man to his praise.

22. Though thou shouldest bray a fool in a mortar among wheat with a pestle, yet will not his foolishness depart from him.

23. Be thou diligent to know the state of thy flocks, and look well to thy herds.

24. For riches are not for ever: and doth the crown endure to every generation?

25. The hay appeareth, and the tender grass sheweth itself, and herbs of the mountains are gathered.

26. The lambs are for thy clothing, and the goats are the price of the field.

27. And thou shalt have goats' milk enough for thy food, for the food of thy household, and for the maintenance for thy maidens.

A crucible for silver . . . Crucibles and furnaces are used to determine the quality of metals, but the worthiness of a man is determined by the extent to which people praise him. He who has earned the good-opinion of people, has also earned the good-opinion of God.

Know well . . . so that you may know what their needs are.

Wealth is not eternal. The verse warns against treating possessions of little value carelessly.

When grass has appeared . . . Verses 25-27 warn against neglecting the care of relatively low-value possessions – you may one day lack your basic necessities and have to sustain yourself on that which you considered valueless. Alternatively, these verses are a metaphor for the ideal approach a Rabbi should take toward his congregation.

PROVERBS 28

1. The wicked flee when no man pursueth: but the righteous are bold as a lion.

2. For the transgression of a land many are the princes thereof: but by a man of understanding and knowledge the state thereof shall be prolonged.

3. A poor man that oppresseth the poor is like a sweeping rain which leaveth no food.

4. They that forsake the law praise the wicked: but such as keep the law contend with them.

5. Evil men understand not judgment: but they that seek the Lord understand all things.

6. Better is the poor that walketh in his uprightness, than he that is perverse in his ways, though he be rich.

7. Whoso keepeth the law is a wise son: but he that is a companion of riotous men shameth his father.

8. He that by usury and unjust gain increaseth his substance, he shall gather it for him that will pity the poor.

9. He that turneth away his ear from hearing the law, even his prayer shall be abomination.

10. Whoso causeth the righteous to go astray in an evil way, he shall fall himself into his own pit: but the upright shall have good things in possession.

<u>The wicked flee . . . (Leviticus 26:36).</u> Their paranoia - a consequence of their atheistic outlook, which allows for death and destruction to occur at random. In contrast, the stalwart faith of the righteous precludes fear, imbuing them instead with the courage of lions. Wickedness generates fear; righteousness brings joy.

<u>It ministers to many.</u> Such a country is destined for destruction. For an oversized government indicates that its leaders' primary concern is not the welfare of the nation, but to exploit their office for personal gain.

<u>Prolonged</u>, or "its punishment is postponed."

<u>A poor man.</u> Referring to an unworthy judge.

<u>Leaves no food</u>, even for himself. A person who obtains wealth through injustice will himself eventually be left destitute.

<u>Those who forsake Torah praise the wicked.</u> As well as their misconstrued ideologies, or those who praise the wicked forsake Torah.

<u>Justice</u>, that is, Godly justice. The wicked do not ponder the heavenly punishment that awaits them and so fail to repent for their sins. Their callousness is due to their denial of Divine Providence and their tendency to ascribe all events to mere coincidence.

Alternatively, the verse teaches that the wicked do not understand the real reason why the wicked succeed in worldly endeavors.

<u>Understand all</u>, the know how to interpret every event as an act of Divine Providence, ascribing nothing to chance.

<u>He who heeds . . .</u> the deeds of one who heeds the Torah are a credit to his father, for people exclaim, "He must have been brought in by a man of

great understanding." In contrast, one who forsakes the Torah to pursue earthly desires cause people to say, "His father must be a boor who never taught him Torah."

<u>Amasses it for the benefit of the poor.</u> Word of his ill-gotten profits will teach the government, who will confiscate them to then use these funds for public works that benefit the poor.

<u>Also . . .</u> not only his requests but also his praise of God is rejected because he has turned away from Torah.

<u>The innocent.</u> His intended victims; or the righteous who guide people to holiness.

11. The rich man is wise in his own conceit; but the poor that hath understanding searcheth him out.

12. When righteous men do rejoice, there is great glory: but when the wicked rise, a man is hidden.

13. He that covereth his sins shall not prosper: but whoso confesseth and forsaketh them shall have mercy.

14. Happy is the man that feareth alway: but he that hardeneth his heart shall fall into mischief.

15. As a roaring lion, and a ranging bear; so is a wicked ruler over the poor people.

16. The prince that wanteth understanding is also a great oppressor: but he that hateth covetousness shall prolong his days.

17. A man that doeth violence to the blood of any person shall flee to the pit; let no man stay him.

18. Whoso walketh uprightly shall be saved: but he that is perverse in his ways shall fall at once.

19. He that tilleth his land shall have plenty of bread: but he that followeth after vain persons shall have poverty enough.

20. A faithful man shall abound with blessings: but he that maketh haste to be rich shall not be innocent.

The rich man considers himself wise. And so feels no need to acquire more wisdom.

But the poor man . . . or "but an understanding poor man sees through him."

There is great glory. God's name is sanctified when the righteous are blessed with success, for under their leadership the voice of evil is silenced.

Men are searched. A wicked ruler searches the homes of his subjects and seizes all valuable possessions, or he searches after those who went into hiding upon his rise to power, or the verse refers to the negative effect a wicked ruler has upon his subjects. His rise to supremacy emboldens so many others to embrace evil that righteous individuals – "men" in the full sense of the word – become scarce, leaving a person no choice but to search after them.

He who cover up . . . This principle applies equally to transgressions committed against either God or men. Confessing our sins is uncovering and renouncing them. It is the path to God's mercy.

Who always fears. God; or a heavenly punishment; or the wicked; or danger; or forgetting the Torah he has learned.

Hates injustice, or "unjust gain" and "robbery" (Exodus 18:21)

Lives long. Will have "length of days."

A man in the grip of blood guilt. Referring to one who has committed murder; or persuaded others to sin.

<u>Flees until the pit.</u> The weight of his sin induces him to commit suicide; or God will cause him to be persecuted until the days of his death.

<u>Do not support him.</u> No one will come to his assistance; or the verse warns against coming to his assistance. Alternatively, it teaches that such an individual will not receive heavenly assistance to repent for his sin.

<u>Will be delivered</u> from the numerous calamities that surround him.

<u>Frivolities;</u> or "empty men" or "false beliefs."

<u>An honest man . . .</u> one who faithfully separates tithes even when no one is looking.

<u>In a rush to get rich</u> and therefore exploits the poor, or commits fraud, or simply spends his entire life running after money.

God's people do not set their sights on material prosperity. God's people seek to be faithful to Him, to be fair and just with other people and to help others. These attitudes lead to God's blessings. Selfish commitment to wealth leads to eventual ruin.

21. To have respect of persons is not good: for for a piece of bread that man will transgress.

22. He that hasteth to be rich hath an evil eye, and considereth not that poverty shall come upon him.

23. He that rebuketh a man afterwards shall find more favour than he that flattereth with the tongue.

24. Whoso robbeth his father or his mother, and saith, It is no transgression; the same is the companion of a destroyer.

25. He that is of a proud heart stirreth up strife: but he that putteth his trust in the Lord shall be made fat.

26. He that trusteth in his own heart is a fool: but whoso walketh wisely, he shall be delivered.

27. He that giveth unto the poor shall not lack: but he that hideth his eyes shall have many a curse.

28. When the wicked rise, men hide themselves: but when they perish, the righteous increase.

A man . . . a judge is liable to become partial to one litigant even if all he received from him was a gift of little value.

Runs headlong after wealth. By not separating tithes; or by not giving charity. The verse refers to a person who, lacking faith in God, becomes obsessed with the fear that he will one day be left totally destitute. Such people usually turn into misers. This is truly unfortunate, however, because miserliness itself begets poverty.

Finds more favor . . . In the eyes of the one he rebuked; or in the eyes of people generally. As a rule, people prefer a man who speaks honestly to one who knows how to flatter his listeners.

We need to be cordial and tactful in confronting others, but we need to face differences honestly. In the long run, confrontation gains more respect than saying simply what the other wants to hear.

His father and mother. Aside from its literal meaning, this refers to a person who persuades others to forsake the Torah. In so doing, he "steals from his father" – God – and "mother" – the community of Israel.

A greedy spirit. One who pursues earthly pleasures; or one who is confident in his own strength and does not fear God; or one who always wants more and is never satisfied with his lot.

PROVERBS 29

1. He, that being often reproved hardeneth his neck, shall suddenly be destroyed, and that without remedy.

2. When the righteous are in authority, the people rejoice: but when the wicked beareth rule, the people mourn.

3. Whoso loveth wisdom rejoiceth his father: but he that keepeth company with harlots spendeth his substance.

4. The king by judgment establisheth the land: but he that receiveth gifts overthroweth it.

5. A man that flattereth his neighbour spreadeth a net for his feet.

6. In the transgression of an evil man there is a snare: but the righteous doth sing and rejoice.

7. The righteous considereth the cause of the poor: but the wicked regardeth not to know it.

8. Scornful men bring a city into a snare: but wise men turn away wrath.

9. If a wise man contendeth with a foolish man, whether he rage or laugh, there is no rest.

10. The bloodthirsty hate the upright: but the just seek his soul.

A man deserving . . . This is fitting punishment for his sin. He stubbornly refused to heal his soul by repenting for his sins, and so his physical wounds prove equally unresponsive to healing.

We can fail to learn through indifference and apathy. Stubbornness can also stand as a barrier to learning, often with disastrous results. Refusal to learn and change is a sin against God.

The people rejoice. Because righteous leaders seek the welfare of the people and evoke Divine supervision.

He who befriends harlots. This includes all those who indiscriminately follow their physical desires.

In the scriptures, wisdom has a definite moral component. A person who has true wisdom does not associate with prostitutes or show other signs of moral illiteracy.

A man of tithes. Referring to a corrupt Judge who "tithes" a shore of the profits in return for acquitting the guilty party; or referring to a Nassi who seizes more than his prescribed portion of crops.

Trapped by his own sin; or a wicked man's sin is a trap "for those who associate with him."

The righteous man sings and rejoices. In gratitude for having avoided the ways of the wicked.

A righteous man knows . . . He is aware of their suffering and knows their needs. Thus, he is kind to them and takes up their cause.

Set a city aflame. By sowing discord among its inhabitants.

The wise mitigate wrath . . . By resolving conflicts between fellow Jews.

<u>When a wise man . . .</u> The verse warns against engaging a foolish man in argument, for regardless of whether the wise man uses anger or humor to make his point, he will not succeed.

<u>The upright seek him out.</u> The upright cherish men of innocence and seek to assist them; or the upright seek out men of innocence to handle their estates for them, because such men are trustworthy; or "the upright pursue them" – the upright pursue the murderous men who cause harm to the innocent. Wicked people cannot stand the presence of righteous people. The righteous become murder victims because their presence witnesses to the guilt of the wicked.

11. A fool uttereth all his mind: but a wise man keepeth it in till afterwards.

12. If a ruler hearken to lies, all his servants are wicked.

13. The poor and the deceitful man meet together: the Lord lighteneth both their eyes.

14. The king that faithfully judgeth the poor, his throne shall be established for ever.

15. The rod and reproof give wisdom: but a child left to himself bringeth his mother to shame.

16. When the wicked are multiplied, transgression increaseth: but the righteous shall see their fall.

17. Correct thy son, and he shall give thee rest; yea, he shall give delight unto thy soul.

18. Where there is no vision, the people perish: but he that keepeth the law, happy is he.

19. A servant will not be corrected by words: for though he understand he will not answer.

20. Seest thou a man that is hasty in his words? there is more hope of a fool than of him.

His fury; or "his thoughts"; or "his earthly desires." Literally, "his spirit."

All his servants become wicked. If one minister tells the ruler a lie in order to find favor in his eyes, all his other ministers will begin doing the same.

The poor and the impoverished man. Referring to individuals who were always poor; or refers to those who were once wealthy but lost their riches.

Meet. The poor and the recently impoverished alike only "meet" the fate which God has decreed for them.

Enlightens them both. This is God delivering them both from the trials of poverty. The verse may also be metaphorically applied to Torah study; "the poor" refers to a complete boor who never studied Torah, while "the impoverished" refers to one who received a Torah education but forgot what he learned.

If such individuals would attempt to study Torah together and beseech God for understanding, he would surely "enlighten" them both.

A neglected youth. A youngster who was spared the rod and did not receive proper guidance from his parents but was rather left to pursue the desires of his heart.

Brings pleasures to your soul . . . in the world to come. For if a righteous man's son is evil, the father's soul is taken out of Gar Eden and into a Gehinnom for him to witness his son's affliction.

In the absence of prophetic vision; or "vision" refers to worthy leaders.

Happy is he who keeps the Torah. Those whose Torah observance is not conditional on the existence of prophets.

A slave. The verse is not meant to be taken literally. Rather, it refers to a litigant who refuses to accept the court's verdict; or to one who is driven by his earthly desires.

People who maintain the laws of life revealed by God are blessed, for they have found the genuine meaning of life. Within this wisdom writing is affirmation of prophetic vision and the law. Thus, a combination of the three major sections of the Hebrew Bible – Law, Prophets and Writings. All three types of inspired literature seek to bring people to know and do God's will so they will have meaning in life. Cautions use of language is necessary to succeed in any area of life. Constant speaking without thinking or listening leads nowhere.

21. He that delicately bringeth up his servant from a child shall have him become his son at the length.

22. An angry man stirreth up strife, and a furious man aboundeth in transgression.

23. A man's pride shall bring him low: but honour shall uphold the humble in spirit.

24. Whoso is partner with a thief hateth his own soul: he heareth cursing, and bewrayeth it not.

25. The fear of man bringeth a snare: but whoso putteth his trust in the Lord shall be safe.

26. Many seek the ruler's favour; but every man's judgment cometh from the Lord.

27. An unjust man is an abomination to the just: and he that is upright in the way is abomination to the wicked.

His slave. Also an allusion to the evil inclination.

An irascible man commits much sin. For his anger blinds him.

He hears the oath but does not tell. He must remain silent when called to give sworn testimony against the thief, since he himself has a hand in the conspiracy.

A man's fears entrap him. His being afraid in difficult times cause him to sin; or his fear of being left penniless hinders him from giving charity.

The verse teaches that it is wrong for a person to feel fear over earthly concerns. This is not contradictory by "Happy is the man who always fears." (Proverbs 28:14) For the latter refers to matters of Torah and Mitzvah observance.

PROVERBS 30

1. The words of Agur the son of Jakeh, even the prophecy: the man spake unto Ithiel, even unto Ithiel and Ucal,

2. Surely I am more brutish than any man, and have not the understanding of a man.

3. I neither learned wisdom, nor have the knowledge of the holy.

4. Who hath ascended up into heaven, or descended? who hath gathered the wind in his fists? who hath bound the waters in a garment? who hath established all the ends of the earth? what is his name, and what is his son's name, if thou canst tell?

5. Every word of God is pure: he is a shield unto them that put their trust in him.

6. Add thou not unto his words, lest he reprove thee, and thou be found a liar.

7. Two things have I required of thee; deny me them not before I die:

8. Remove far from me vanity and lies: give me neither poverty nor riches; feed me with food convenient for me:

9. Lest I be full, and deny thee, and say, Who is the Lord? or lest I be poor, and steal, and take the name of my God in vain.

10. Accuse not a servant unto his master, lest he curse thee, and thou be found guilty.

11. There is a generation that curseth their father, and doth not bless their mother.

Agur son of Yakeh. Some say this was one of King Solomon's pseudonyms. Agur is derived from Le'agor, "to gather." King Solomon gathered more wisdom than any other human being.

Yakeh is from the verb Le'aki, "to vomit." After gathering all this wisdom, King Solomon spit it out, when certain of his actions caused him to lose his great wisdom.

The prophecy of the man. The continuation of the verse figuratively explains how King Solomon came to "vomit" or lose his wisdom.

"The man" – King Solomon became too confident in his wisdom and mistakenly considered himself exempt from the restrictions the Torah places on Jewish Kings.

Thus, he disregarded the verse, "(the King) must not accumulate many horses . . . He must not have many wives, so that they do not make his heart go astray. He should likewise not accumulate very much silver and gold" (Deuteronomy 17:16,17). Solomon felt confident that he would remain faithful to God despite these excesses. However, King Solomon was proven wrong. At it is written, "Solomon had 700 royal wives and 300 concubines, and his wives turned his heart away (from God.) In his old age, they turned his heart toward other gods, and he was not as wholeheartedly devoted to God his Lord as his father David had been . . . God became angry with Solomon, for his heart turned away from God, Lord of Israel" (I Kings 11:3,9).

Ithiel and Ukhal. According to those who say that Agur son of Yakeh was the name of a prominent sage in King Solomon's time, Ithiel and Ukhal were either Agur's disciples or colleagues, to whom Agur addressed his compositions. Agur repeated Ithiel's name in his introductory remarks out of respect for Ithiel, the greater of the two.

Although I had not learned . . . knowledge of the holy. King Solomon in essence said, "Initially I thought that the Torah's prohibition against taking too many wives was merely a preventative measure lest a King turn away from God. Little did I realize that God, in His great wisdom knew in all certainty that this outcome was inevitable."

Who ascended . . . As did Moses when he ascended to heaven and received the Torah from the angels.

Who gathered wind . . . referring to Exodus 9:8.

Who tied up the water . . . referring to Exodus 15:8. God performs this miracle in answer to Moses' prayer.

Who established all the ends of the earth? The foundations of the earth were only made firm when Moses erected the Tabernacle, with or when, the Torah was given to Israel.

What is his name or son's name? A theatrical question, since the entire verse clearly alludes to Moses. "In light of Moses' awesome wisdom, how could I have disregarded the restrictions placed upon me by the Torah? King Soloman asked.

God's every statement is pure. "Since not a single word in the Torah is superfluous, I should have heeded its warnings", King Solomon reflected; or since the Torah's commandments are analogous to refined gold, it is not fitting to waste one's time on other pursuits.

He is a shield . . . I errored in believing that my wisdom would protect me from mishap, for only he who places his trust in God's Torah is truly protected.

Do not add to His words. They are inherently pure and so need no modifications.

Dr. Gilbert H. Edwards, Sr.

<u>Lest He demonstrates it to you</u>. That as a consequence of your "adding to His word" you are guilty of transgression.

<u>I ask of you</u>. The speaker now addresses God.

<u>Before I die.</u> "Give them to me throughout my life."

<u>Who is God?</u> As in Deuteronomy 8:12-14.

<u>Defiling the name of my God</u>. By taking false oaths in order to clear himself of theft charges or feeling bitter toward God for making his lot so meager.

<u>Which is a worse sin,</u> "Lest I have my fill and renounce (you), saying, "Who is God?" or Lest I become poor and turn to steading and defiling the name of my God?"

<u>The second is worse,</u> for we find that God overlooks idolatry, but He does not overlook the sin of defiling His name. As it is written (Ezekiel 20:39), "As for you, O House of Israel; let each man go worship his idols . . . but do not profane my holy name."

Do not denounce . . . The verse warns against spreading slander, especially when the victim is bound to suffer repercussion. On a deeper level, it warns against accusing any man before the Master of the world. Even if he be a most wicked individual.

This principle is derived from the Prophet Hosea who suggested to God that he destroy Israel and replace them with another nation. God punished Hosea by ordering him to marry a harlot.

Even if it be. "Do not spread slander" about any of these generations even though their wickedness is great.

12. here is a generation that are pure in their own eyes, and yet is not washed from their filthiness.

13. There is a generation, O how lofty are their eyes! and their eyelids are lifted up.

14. There is a generation, whose teeth are as swords, and their jaw teeth as knives, to devour the poor from off the earth, and the needy from among men.

15. The horseleach hath two daughters, crying, Give, give. There are three things that are never satisfied, yea, four things say not, It is enough:

16. The grave; and the barren womb; the earth that is not filled with water; and the fire that saith not, It is enough.

17. The eye that mocketh at his father, and despiseth to obey his mother, the ravens of the valley shall pick it out, and the young eagles shall eat it.

18. There be three things which are too wonderful for me, yea, four which I know not:\

19. The way of an eagle in the air; the way of a serpent upon a rock; the way of a ship in the midst of the sea; and the way of a man with a maid.

20. Such is the way of an adulterous woman; she eateth, and wipeth her mouth, and saith, I have done no wickedness.

21. For three things the earth is disquieted, and for four which it cannot bear:

22. For a servant when he reigneth; and a fool when he is filled with meat;

Excrement. Euphemism for sexual promiscuity (Ezra Verse 16).

<u>The Leech.</u> A metaphor for the graves, or for the corrupt ways of the four generations mentioned in verses 11-14; or for Gehinuim.

<u>Give and give.</u> Referring to Gan Eden and Gehinnom – one says, "give me the souls of the righteous." While others say, "give me the souls of the wicked!" Both have plenty of room for the souls of all future generations.

<u>The Nether World.</u> Untimely death awaits the generation "that curses its Father and does not bless its Mother." In fulfillment of Exodus 21:17.

<u>A barren womb.</u> Infidelity will be the punishment of the generation that "is not cleaned of its own excrement" – i.e., commits sexual transgressions.

<u>A land thirsty for water.</u> Severe drought will humble the generation "that is so very haughty and conceited."

<u>A fire</u> from heaven will descend and engulf those who oppress "the poor of the land and the destitute among men"; or "Fire" refers to severe ways. Alternatively, the fires of Gehinnom.

<u>Aging, as in Genesis 49:11</u>, where it means "gathering. As the "gatherings" or "wrinkles", or a mother's face.

<u>The way of the eagle . . .</u> Just as the eagle, the snake and the ship leave no trail, so illicit sexual relations are easily concealed.

<u>Such is the way . . .</u> King Solomon fails to understand the mentality of those who commit adultery, for although they may succeed in concealing their sin from human beings, how can they possibly expect to evade God?

<u>A boor who has his fill of food.</u> His apparent security and comfort prompts others to emulate his ways.

23. For an odious woman when she is married; and an handmaid that is heir to her mistress.

24. There be four things which are little upon the earth, but they are exceeding wise:

25. The ants are a people not strong, yet they prepare their meat in the summer;

26. The conies are but a feeble folk, yet make they their houses in the rocks;

27. The locusts have no king, yet go they forth all of them by bands;

28. The spider taketh hold with her hands, and is in kings' palaces.

29. There be three things which go well, yea, four are comely in going:

30. A lion which is strongest among beasts, and turneth not away for any;

31. A greyhound; an he goat also; and a king, against whom there is no rising up.

32. If thou hast done foolishly in lifting up thyself, or if thou hast thought evil, lay thine hand upon thy mouth.

33. Surely the churning of milk bringeth forth butter, and the wringing of the nose bringeth forth blood: so the forcing of wrath bringeth forth strife.

An odious woman taken by a man. A harlot who legitimates an illicit pregnancy by marrying a man. By sinning and evading punishment, she emboldens others to follow her example.

They are extremely wise. God endowed them with wisdom so that mankind would learn from them.

Ants . . . God endowed the ant with diligence, so that the indolent would take note and emulate them.

<u>Rabbits</u> . . . God endowed the rabbit with perseverance as a lesson to those who feel intimidated by the sheer depth and breadth of the Torah one must study.

<u>Locusts</u> . . . By instinctively joining other members of its species, the feeble locusts become an invincible force. It is in man's best interest to do the same.

<u>The spider</u> . . . The spider prefers the insects caught in the web it wove with its own hands to the delicacies it can garner from a King's table. A person, too, should try to subsist from the fruits of his own labor rather than rely on the generosity of others.

<u>There are three</u> . . . These verses allude to the qualities necessary to be a baal teshurah, one who has wholeheartedly repented from his sins. He must be as brave as a lion, since it stands to reason that he will be ridiculed by his peers for wanting to follow the ways of the Torah; swift as a greyhound in fulfilling the positive commandments; and as wary as a he-goat, regarding the negative commandments.

If he keeps in mind that the Torah, or "the King whom one does dare attack" is protecting him, he will not be intimidated by anyone.

<u>Because of your desire for honor</u>, or "If you have been disgraced (respond) with dignity."

<u>For pressure on milk</u> . . . This verse explains why a person who has been humiliated should "put his hand over his mouth" and remain silent.

There are three reasons why people answer when insulted: (1) to prove that they are better than the instigator, (2) to prove the insult false and (3) to deter the instigator from repeating his offense in the future. By mentioning the butter churning process, the verse invalidates the first reason for answering back. To make butter, the milk must be covered with a lid; and just as butter is unquestionably a product of superior quality, so too a person who "puts a lid on his mouth" in the face of insult demonstrates that he is of far more noble character than the lowly instigator.

<u>Regarding the second reason.</u> The verse teaches that just as a nosebleed is best left untouched, so silence is the way to block the defamatory damage of an insult.

<u>Finally.</u> The verse negates the third reason by pointing out that "pressure on anger produces quarrel" – an angry response only elicits further quarrel and further insults. Silence on the other hand, ensures that this outrage will not be repeated.

PROVERBS 31

1. The words of king Lemuel, the prophecy that his mother taught him.

2. What, my son? and what, the son of my womb? and what, the son of my vows?

3. Give not thy strength unto women, nor thy ways to that which destroyeth kings.

4. It is not for kings, O Lemuel, it is not for kings to drink wine; nor for princes strong drink:

5. Lest they drink, and forget the law, and pervert the judgment of any of the afflicted.

6. Give strong drink unto him that is ready to perish, and wine unto those that be of heavy hearts.

7. Let him drink, and forget his poverty, and remember his misery no more.

8. Open thy mouth for the dumb in the cause of all such as are appointed to destruction.

9. Open thy mouth, judge righteously, and plead the cause of the poor and needy.

Many say this is another of King Solomon's pseudonym: "Lemuel" is a compound of Lamo el, literally "for God."

<u>The prophecy with which his mother rebuked him</u> on the same night that King Solomon completed the construction of the first temple. He married Pharoah's daughter (I Kings 7:8).

The celebrations in honor of these two events coincided with the latter surpassing the former. At that moment, God considered destroying Jerusalem. King Solomon was called Lemuel – a compound of Lamah Lo el, which means, "What does he need God for?" The next morning, the timid sacrifice was only offered in the fourth hour of the day. The Jewish people were most despondent, as they would have wanted to offer the sacrifice earlier on the day marking the temple's inauguration. But King Solomon was still asleep, and out of fear of the King, no one dared to wake him.

Finally, they turned to his mother, Bathsheba, who promptly woke her son and rebuked him. (Numbers 10:4) The extent of King Solomon's respect for his mother is evident in the fact that he regarded her words of rebuke as prophetic.

<u>Your strength to women.</u> Excessive sexual activity saps a man's strength, or let your ways . . . Do not digress from the traditional, moderate and discreet conduct exhibited by Kings.

<u>Undetermined the judgement of all the poor.</u> They are always the victims of injustice because they are meek and helpless, whereas the rich use their influence to fight back.

<u>The forlorn.</u> Referring to the wicked, or to the poor. Civil leaders cannot afford to have their judgment and actions impaired from misuse of alcohol. They should refrain from those things which work against justice being done.

<u>Speak up for the dumb.</u> If a litigant proves incapable of presenting his case, the Judge must assist him.

<u>Orphans.</u> Whose help has passed them by. Alternatively, (literally, "passing away") refers to those who confuse one idea for another and prove capable of arguing their case coherently.

10. Who can find a virtuous woman? for her price is far above rubies.

11. The heart of her husband doth safely trust in her, so that he shall have no need of spoil.

12. She will do him good and not evil all the days of her life.

13. She seeketh wool, and flax, and worketh willingly with her hands.

14. She is like the merchants' ships; she bringeth her food from afar.

15. She riseth also while it is yet night, and giveth meat to her household, and a portion to her maidens.

16. She considereth a field, and buyeth it: with the fruit of her hands she planteth a vineyard.

17. She girdeth her loins with strength, and strengtheneth her arms.

18. She perceiveth that her merchandise is good: her candle goeth not out by night.

19. She layeth her hands to the spindle, and her hands hold the distaff.

20. She stretcheth out her hand to the poor; yea, she reacheth forth her hands to the needy.

<u>A woman of valor.</u> "A woman of valor" may be a metaphor for Divine presence, or for a Jew's conscience; or for his natural desire to gather knowledge; or for the soul; or for Sarah the matriarch or for the Torah.

Repays him with good not evil. She is not vindictive-repaying him a good turn in kind, but not reciprocating when he acts unkindly towards her; or she is good to him, never bad.

Looks for wool and linen. Whatever her trade, she strives to excel in it. She is also self-motivated, since buying thread was traditionally not a woman's job.

Bringing her food from afar. She helps her husband bear the burden of supporting a household by selling her hand and work in distant market where greater profits may be earned.

Rises while it is still night-time. She does not neglect her domestic responsibilities but rises before dawn and nurtures her household.

Considers . . . She sets her mind on a goal and does not deviate from it until she achieves it.

With the fruit of her handiwork. She buys the field, works the hand, and then spend the profits of her handiwork to plant a vine.

Perceives . . . When she perceives that her trade is profitable, she will work late into the night; or the verse teaches that a woman of valor is not satisfied with merely earning enough for her own needs. Instinctively, she perceives that she should donate some of her labor to "good" causes such as charity and acts of kindness. To this end, she works extra hours at night.

Extends her hands . . . Despite her success in traditionally made occupations, she does not shun womanly tasks such as weaving.

Spreads out her palm . . . extends her hands . . . She gives generously to the poor who ask for food, and also to those too ashamed to ask for help.

21. She is not afraid of the snow for her household: for all her household are clothed with scarlet.

22. She maketh herself coverings of tapestry; her clothing is silk and purple.

23. Her husband is known in the gates, when he sitteth among the elders of the land.

24. She maketh fine linen, and selleth it; and delivereth girdles unto the merchant.

25. Strength and honour are her clothing; and she shall rejoice in time to come.

26. She openeth her mouth with wisdom; and in her tongue is the law of kindness.

27. She looketh well to the ways of her household, and eateth not the bread of idleness.

28. Her children arise up, and call her blessed; her husband also, and he praiseth her.

29. Many daughters have done virtuously, but thou excellest them all.

30. Favour is deceitful, and beauty is vain: but a woman that feareth the Lord, she shall be praised.

31. Give her of the fruit of her hands; and let her own works praise her in the gates.

Crimson wool. (Exodus 25:4) The dye itself retained heat.

Dark-red wool. (Exodus 25:4) the verse teaches that her prosperity is proof that God has blessed her work.

Her husband is renowned in the gates. As a direct consequence of her unwavering support for her husband's Torah study, he becomes one of the most prominent scholars in the land; or the graceful clothing she makes for him causes him to stand out among his fees not llow scholars.

<u>Delivers a belt to the merchant.</u> She even earns by selling to the merchants.

<u>Laughs.</u> Lack of anxiety.

<u>To the last day.</u> A woman of valor has no reason to fear heavenly judgement; or does not dread death for she knows that she will be remembered for her righteous deeds; or because she knows the extent of the great eternal reward awaiting her in the world to come.

<u>The Law of Living Kindness. . .</u> She teaches and encourages others to do acts of kindness on behalf of their fellow men.

<u>Observes the conduct . . .</u> And when necessary, she sets them right.

<u>Does not partake of the bread of idleness.</u> She does not linger over her food in the manner of the indolent, but eats quickly and returns to her duties.

<u>Give her . . .</u> that is, "Praise her for the fruit of her labor."

<u>Her own deeds . . .</u> Her virtuous deeds will cause her fame to spread far and wide.

The accomplishments of a wise and industrious woman are magnificent to behold and a source of strength and encouragement to all who know her. A wise woman's potential reaches out to many fields of endeavor. Women may play many roles in a successful family relationship. This appears to be a composite picture of the ideal wife and mother. One woman could hardly perform all the functions mentioned within one day. The woman is equally active in home and business duties.

She is trusted by her husband and seeks to help him at all times. She works hard, makes difficult decisions, earns and invests money well, is compassionate and helpful to the needy, is prepared for the future and has wisdom to teach other people. She has earned a high reputation in her family, in the business world, and in the community. All of this is possible because her life is centered on God.

The Bible thus challenges women to use their talents in as many areas as possible to bring honor to God, their family and themselves. I personally do not seek to bring a guilt trip on the woman who cannot succeed in all these areas. Few can succeed, but all should have the opportunity to try.

ACKNOWLEDGEMENTS

I want to thank Minister Mark Stansberry, Sr.
for the cover design of this book.
and
I gracefully continue to thank my long time Secretary
Pastor L. Evon McDowell who has labored with me, as my
personal typist through Bible College and Seminary.
She is also my personal Pastoral Assistant.

Printed in the United States
by Baker & Taylor Publisher Services